DISCOVER DERRY

BRIAN LACEY

Brian Lacey was born in Dublin in 1949 and educated at University College, Dublin, where he studied Celtic archaeology and early Irish history. From 1974 to 1986 he was a lecturer in Local Studies at Magee University College in Derry. During that period he directed a series of rescue excavations at sites in the centre of Derry, and also the Donegal archaeological survey in 1980-1. From 1986 to 1998 he was head of Derry City Council's Heritage and Museum Service. During this period he established four local museums as well as other heritage facilities (the Tower Museum, opened in 1992, is the only institution to date to have been both British and Irish Museum of the Year). He is now Programme Manager of the Discovery Programme (an archaeological research institution) in Dublin. He has contributed articles and chapters to various historical and archaeological books and journals. He edited the *Archaeological Survey of County Donegal,* published in 1983. Other publications include *Historic Derry* (1988) and *The Siege of Derry* (1989), both in the Eason's Irish Heritage Series. His other books are: *Siege City: The Story of Derry and Londonderry* (Blackstaff Press, 1990), *Colum Cille and the Columban Tradition* (Four Courts Press, 1997) and *The Life of Colum Cille by Manus O'Donnell* (Four Courts Press, 1998).

Discover DERRY

BRIAN LACEY

THE O'BRIEN PRESS LTD.

DUBLIN

First published 1999 by The O'Brien Press Ltd.,
20 Victoria Road, Dublin 6, Ireland.
Tel. +353 1 4923333; Fax. +353 1 4922777
e-mail: books@obrien.ie
website: http://www.obrien.ie

ISBN: 0-86278-596-0

British Library Cataloguing-in-publication Data

A catalogue record for this title is available from the British Library

1 2 3 4 5 6 7 8 9 10
99 00 01 02 03 04 05 06 07

The O'Brien Press receives
assistance from

The Arts Council
An Chomhairle Ealaíon

Layout and design: The O'Brien Press Ltd.
Cover and inside photographs: Robert Vance
Map of modern Derry: Design Image
Colour separations: C&A Print Services, Dublin
Printing: Zure S.A.

ACKNOWLEDGEMENTS

The author and publisher thank the following for permission to reproduce photographs:
Derry City Council Heritage and Museum Service, cover painting (top), 35; The National
Museum of Ireland, 17; Public Records Office, London, 23; The Honourable The Irish Socie-
ty's Papers, Corporation of London Records Office, London, 26; The British Museum, 31;
Ickworth, The Bristol Collection, The National Trust, NT Photo Library, 41; the Trustees of
the National Museums and Galleries of Northern Ireland, 40; courtesy David Bigger, 53; The
Trustees of the Imperial War Museum, London, 54; Pacemaker, Belfast, 63; SDLP Press
Office, 64; The Playhouse, Derry, 94.

While every effort has been made to clear copyright, if any oversight has inadvertently occurred
the publishers request the holder of such copyright to contact them immediately.

For Katie

CONTENTS

PART ONE: THE HISTORY OF THE CITY

PART TWO: GUIDE TO THE HISTORIC CITY

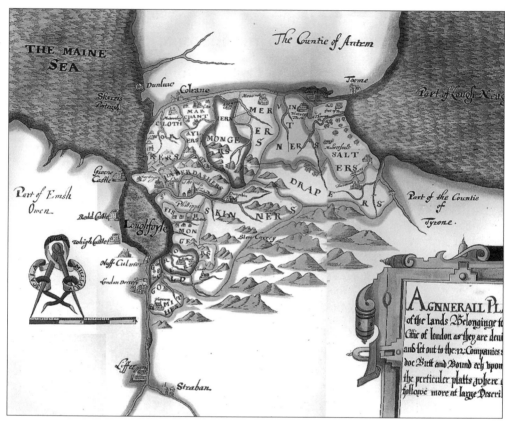

The county of Londonderry or Derry, c.1625.

THE HISTORY OF THE CITY

Discover Derry

Since the late 1960s Derry has experienced profound social trauma and has also undergone a period of extraordinary physical change. The built-up area of the city is now nearly ten times the size it was thirty years ago – most of the buildings in the city date since the 1970s. It seems paradoxical that this beautiful and historical place has for such a long time been a byword for political and social instability and violence. Derry is a very ancient and, equally, a very new city. In some ways it can be said to be one of the oldest continuously inhabited places in Ireland, or at least one of the few such places for which we have a reasonably continuous documented history.

Our earliest contemporary records for Derry date back as far as the late sixth or early seventh century, but various legends and archaeological finds made within the confines of the city would suggest that the area was inhabited long before that. The modern city, of course, has spread well beyond the hill of Derry which gave its name to the original settlement as well as to the present enlarged urban area. Nowadays, the suburbs have spread across many of the small hills which encircle the hill of Derry on the west bank of the river Foyle – the hill from which the whole city has grown. These hills assumed their shape in the closing period of the last Ice Age.

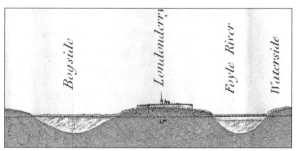

Cross-section through city and river Foyle.

At that time (between 175,000 BC and 15,000 BC) glaciers, originating both in the mountains of Donegal and as far away as Scotland, spread outwards, eventually reaching Derry and its vicinity. The planing action of the ice as it relentlessly moved forwards and backwards over thousands of years gave these hills their distinctive rounded shape, as well as leaving behind deposits of gravel and sand which would eventually be exploited for the construction of the city's buildings. Many of the city's older buildings and especially the seventeenth-century defensive walls are constructed from the deposits of schist which lie close to the surface of the ground and appear as outcrops and quarries at a number of locations in and around the city. Basically, there is just one layer of rock underneath the city. One of the jokes which people make about Derry's controversial past is that the simplest part of it, paradoxically, is its geology – once human beings arrive on the scene controversy tends to take over.

The city lies on a beautiful bend in the river Foyle. About five to six thousand years ago the river would have run around both sides of the hill of Derry making it into an island. However, the western channel partially dried out in ancient times leaving behind a marshy, 'boggy' valley – the Bogside – which acquired its own fame in due course. The Elizabethan Sir Henry Docwra aptly described Derry's geographical situation:

> 'It lies in [the] form of a bow bent, whereof the bog[-side] is the string and the river the bow.'

Many places claim to be historic and, in so far as everywhere in the world – even the most recent housing development – has a history of some sort, that claim can be justified. However, some places are undoubtedly more historic than others. Derry can truly claim to be such a place, whether one is talking about the sheer length of that history (in strict terms getting on for at least fourteen hundred years), or about the complexity, drama and significance of that history. It is often asserted that for the last seventy years or so Derry has been a border city. But in many ways it has been a border settlement throughout its long history, located on the edge of the territory of one population group or another which was in conflict, or at least competition, with its neighbours. This frontier characteristic of the city is almost a structural phenomenon and derives as much from its physical location on the banks of the wide and fast-flowing river Foyle, as from the political associations of those who have lived there, or live there still.

Derry – The oak grove

The city has variously been known (as far back as we have records), as Daire Calgach, Doire Cholmcille, Londonderry and Derry, as well as a number of other variations of these names. The common element linking them is an Irish word, *Daire* or *Doire* (anglicised as Derry) referring to an ancient oak grove. Oak trees probably arrived in Derry about five thousand years ago as part of the ongoing changes in vegetation and forest cover which followed after the Ice Age. The Derry oak grove gradually acquired a ritual significance, as did oak trees all over the Celtic parts of Europe. This eventually resulted in the naming of Derry after what we can presume was a distinctive grove on the hillside overlooking the river Foyle. There is some circumstantial evidence to suggest that during the Iron Age, between about 800 BC and AD 500, the oaks on the hill of Derry may have had a ritual function and that possibly a fortification there (no evidence of which has yet been found) may have served as a stronghold for some of the local kings.

The ancient monastery

Archaeological objects and monuments have been found in, or close to, the city dating to the Mesolithic Period (c.7,000 BC to c.4,000 BC), the Neolithic Period (c.4,000 BC to c.2,500 BC), the Bronze Age (c.2,500 BC to c.800 BC) and also the Iron Age (c.800 BC to c.AD 500). Strictly speaking, the history of Derry can be said to have started with the foundation of the Early Christian monastic church there, probably in the second half of the sixth century. The date of 546 is often given as the founding year, but it is now generally recognised that this was determined inaccurately by later medieval chroniclers (probably in the twelfth century), and cannot be relied upon. It is also accepted now that questions can be raised about the alleged role played by St Colmcille (also known as Columba), who is traditionally said to have been the founder of the monastery. Genuinely early records suggest the name of an alternative founder who is known to us by the long patronymic form of his name as Fiachra mac Ciárain mac Ainmerech mac Sétna. (As one wag remarked, 'with a name like that is it any wonder that the man's role in the foundation of the city was forgotten about?') There are also several chronological problems which complicate the story further. The church in Derry was probably not founded until about 590, but what is clear is that the church or monastery of Derry was established by the leading local dynasty, the Cenél Conaill, of which Colmcille and Fiachra were important members, and that other members of this family played a decisive role in the development of the settlement there for the next five centuries at least. The legends narrating what was believed to have been the story of the foundation of the monastery by St

Colmcille were probably developed as dynastic propaganda in later times when the Cenél Conaill came under pressure from their neighbours, the even more powerful dynasty known as the Cenél nEógain. Whatever about their historicity, these legends give a fascinating insight into the beliefs and politics of the time.

The legends tell us that Colmcille (who was born in Donegal c.521 and died on Iona in 597) was a student at the monastery of Glasnevin, now a suburb of Dublin. A terrible plague broke out and the students were sent back to their homelands to protect them from contagion.

St Colmcille.

Colmcille went north, was ordained a priest on the way, and eventually arrived in Derry where the king, Aed mac Ainmerech, is said to have had his fortification. (In fact, Aed was a generation later than Colmcille and if he was involved in the foundation of the monastery, it would have been established much later. This suggestion of a later date for the founding of the monastery would also fit with some of the other better-established facts.)

The legends also describe how the king offered the site to Colmcille as a suitable location for a monastery. The monk refused at first but subsequently accepted the offer. The first thing he did was to set fire to the site in what was, in effect, a rite of exorcism. However, when the fire spread and threatened to burn the grove of oak trees, Colmcille, who is said to have loved these trees very much, intervened, composing a famous prayer in Latin: *Noli Pater Indulgere* (Father, do not allow)

> Father, keep under
> The tempest and thunder,
> Lest we should be shattered
> By Thy lightning's shafts scattered ...

In medieval times it was believed that the recitation of this prayer would ensure special protection from the damaging effects of thunder and lightning. The story about the initial burning of the site, the special regard shown for the oak trees and the protections offered from the forces of nature all hint at a pre-Christian ritual significance for Derry (although there is no hard evidence to back up this theory). This would be very much in keeping with other similar Celtic sites, for example, Dubrovnik, the name of which is also based on a derivation of the word for 'oak tree'.

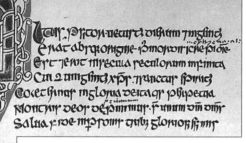

Part of a hymn attributed to St Colmcille.

Whatever the truth, there are other hints that the oaks, among other types of trees in Derry, were surrounded by taboos for a thousand years following the foundation of the monastery there. For example, according to the Annals, in 1188 a Donegal aristocrat who was cutting firewood in Derry in apparent violation of these taboos was killed by 'a miracle of Colmcille'. A medieval poet put words into the mouth of the saint to warn against any such misdeeds. Speaking from his monastery on the island of Iona in the Scottish Hebrides, Colmcille is supposed to have said:

> 'Though truly I'm afraid
> Of death itself and Hell
> I'm frankly more afraid
> Of an axe-sound, back in Derry.'

All of these stories have a Christian veneer but it seems probable that their true significance lies in the ancient primitive beliefs which had survived from pagan times.

We can be certain that the monastery of Derry was founded before the early seventh century and that it was connected, by family and other ties, to the great confederation of churches in various parts of Ireland and Britain which was linked to Colmcille's main establishment on Iona. There are patchy historical records for the first few centuries of its existence, which seem to demonstrate that during this period Derry was a relatively quiet backwater. There are reports of two, or at most three, raiding expeditions by bands of

Vikings in the ninth and tenth centuries, but the settlement does not appear to have been too badly damaged on any of these occasions. It seems that it was not until the early tenth century that Derry began to acquire a greater status (probably along with greater wealth) and to play a more active role in the wider Columban monastic world. Throughout this period the affairs of Derry were dominated by members of the Cenél Conaill dynasty. However, increasingly the settlement was being surrounded by the Cenél nEógain who were capturing the neighbouring territories. By the eleventh century, and probably for a lot longer, Derry was no more than a Cenél Conaill island set in an advancing Cenél nEógain sea.

The monastic 'town'

In 1083 the powerful Domnall Ua Lochlainn became leader of the Cenél nEógain. He set about dominating and taking possession of everything, everyone and every place he could possibly manage. At some point (we don't have an exact date), he took control of Derry, breaching all its previous traditions and associations as a Cenél Conaill settlement. Domnall moved his 'capital' into Derry and eventually died there in 1121. Despite this upheaval, Derry benefited enormously from its association with the Ua Lochlainn kings. They were among the most powerful political figures in the Ireland of their day and competed vigorously for the title and appurtenances of the almost unattainable office of *Ard-rí*, the 'High-kingship' of Ireland. As the twelfth century advanced we find numerous references to the vitality of the secular as well as the ecclesiastical settlement in Derry, and hints of its bustling social and economic life and of its wealth. In 1150, with the arrival of a new abbot, Flaithbertach O'Brolcháin, Derry acquired unprecedented status as the headquarters of the Columban *familia* – the confederation of churches associated with the cult of St Colmcille. New buildings were erected in the settlement, especially the 'great church' or Tempull Mór which would eventually be recognised as the cathedral of the diocese of Derry, an area representing the contemporary authority of the Ua Lochlainn kings. By this stage, Derry must have been as close as anything was in Gaelic Ireland to fulfilling the definition of a 'town'.

We know that there was a great school and scriptorium associated with the monastery as there are various references to lectors and senior lectors in the contemporary literature and a number of literary works and books were produced or preserved there. There is also a spate of propaganda poetry and verse written around this time about Derry. These praises of the settlement were invariably put into the mouth of its patron saint, Colmcille:

> In perfect elegant Derry,
> There's not a leaf upon the ground,
> Above each one of which,
> Two virgin angels can't be found.

And again:

> If all parts of Scotland were mine,
> From its centre, right out to its seas;
> One house plot in Derry, so fine,
> Would, truthfully, me better please.

Among the most highly-prized books in twelfth-century Derry was the *Soiscél Martain*, the 'Gospel Book of St Martin'. This was treated as a most important relic and there were several legends to explain its origins.

> Then Colmcille went on a pilgrimage to Tours [in France] of Saint Martin. He went to the flagstone beneath which Martin was buried. He lifted the stone from the tomb and he found a book of the gospels upon Martin's neck. Martin and that book had been buried in the earth for a hundred years but God had preserved the book for Colmcille so that it was no better on the first day it was made than at that time. And by the will of God and of Martin, Colmcille took the book back with him to Derry, as Martin himself had promised at the time of his death ...

The *Soiscél Martain* was lost in a battle in the 1180s when it was used as a talisman or semi-magical protective device. We do not know exactly what this book was but recently it has been suggested that it can be identified with the surviving manuscript known as the Cathach of Colmcille, which comprises part of a copy of the Psalms and is the oldest Irish manuscript in existence. The Cathach, which was itself used throughout the Middle Ages as a talisman by the Donegal aristocratic family the O'Donnells, is now preserved in the Royal Irish Academy in Dublin. Tradition has it that the Cathach was written by St Colmcille himself, and scholars agree that it could indeed date to the end of the sixth century, before the saint's death. Thus there is no scientific reason for doubting the traditional ascription to the hand of the saint, although it has to be said that there is no scientific proof of its origins either.

Various other treasure items and relics are mentioned in the sources as being located in Derry in the Middle Ages, including St Mobhí's belt.

The Cathach shrine.

> **Saint Mobhí's inflexible belt,**
> **It was not supple like the rushes in a lake.**
> **It was never loosened for greediness,**
> **Nor tightened around anything fake.**

The last line of the verse suggests that the belt may have been a relic on which oaths were sworn. Again, we do not know exactly what form the belt took but it may have resembled the object known as the Moylough Belt-shrine which is now housed in the National Museum of Ireland in Dublin.

Decline and change

By the end of the twelfth century two events had occurred which were to affect the fortunes of Derry to a considerable degree. Various reforms in the Church throughout Ireland, some of them consequent on the arrival of the Normans from 1169 onwards, meant that the Columban *familia* began to disintegrate as a significant ecclesiastical institution. Likewise, the collapse of the Ua Lochlainns' power around the same time meant that Derry was no longer regarded as the centre of political influence that it once had been.

Ireland itself was undergoing profound change at this time as a result of the Norman 'invasion'. Norman expeditions visited Derry on several occasions at the close of the twelfth and the beginning of the thirteenth centuries. The decline in Derry's importance was not immediately apparent, however. For instance, by the middle of the thirteenth century the seat of the diocese had been relocated to the 'city' of Derry from its former base in Maghera, County Derry. There continue to be references to Derry, and especially to its monastery, throughout the later Middle Ages. Early in the thirteenth century the monastery had adopted the Augustinian rule. We know quite a lot about it from the records of a visit made there in 1397 by John Colton, the Archbishop of Armagh. Among his various actions in Derry, Colton had to formulate a set of rules for the moral guidance of the Augustinian Abbey. Among these was the instruction that the abbot should cease to cohabit with his concubine.

Coat-of-arms of the city of Derry.

Earlier in the same century, in 1311, the king of England, Edward II, had granted lands at Derry to Richard de Burgo, the Earl of Ulster. De Burgo had built an enormous castle at a place then called Northburgh (now Greencastle, County Donegal), at the entrance to Lough Foyle about thirty miles north of Derry. He may have intended to develop the settlement at Derry, perhaps as a proper town. However, nothing lasting came of the de Burgo involvement with Derry except perhaps the skeleton on the city's coat-of-arms. According to a long-standing tradition, the origins of which are now lost, this skeleton is supposed to represent the figure of Walter de Burgo who was starved to death. The incident occurred during a family feud when he was immured or blocked up, while still alive, inside the walls of the castle at Northburgh. 'Walter', as the skeleton is popularly known, is still something of a local character and frequently turns up at festival events and civic occasions.

Cathedral and castle

Not much is known about the situation in Derry during the fifteenth century. In 1469 a petition was sent by the local bishop to Pope Paul II. It seems that the cathedral was in poor condition. The pope, in reply, granted an indulgence 'of seven years and seven quarantines of

enjoined penance to all who, being truly penitent and having con-
fessed ... give alms for such rebuilding, restoration and maintenance'
of the cathedral church. Sometime around the end of that century or
the beginning of the following one, a small tower-house castle was
built in Derry for the lords of the neighbouring territory of Tír Conaill
– the O'Donnells. The castle was actually built by the O'Doherty
family of Inishowen (now in County Donegal) for their O'Donnell
overlords in 'consideration ... of certain duties'. The land on which
the castle was built had been bought from the local Ua Lochlainn
family for the princely sum of 'twenty cows'. These Ua Lochlainns
were probably the impoverished descendants of the twelfth-century
kings of the same name who ruled from Derry. From one or two other
hints it seems possible that the O'Donnells, and particularly the
great Manus O'Donnell (b. c.1490, d. 1563), contemplated some sort
of minor renaissance for Derry. We know that there was a pilgrimage
route in Derry around this time, from the riverside near the castle to
the area of the cathedral church, and this, among other things,
would have brought a certain amount of income to the settlement.
The castle, at any rate, survived until well into the seventeenth century when it was used as a gunpowder and ammunition magazine for
the plantation city. The building is still commemorated by a number
of street names as well as by the Castle and Magazine gates which cut
through the city walls. A more concrete reminder is the O'Doherty
Tower – the externally visible section of the Tower Museum. This
building was erected in 1986 but was designed in the style of a
sixteenth-century Irish tower-house in commemoration of the
medieval castle. It is built close to the site of the 'original' castle and
is a very dramatic example of the popular need to make 'invisible history' visible.

The English arrive

Again, little is known about Derry in the first half of the sixteenth
century but there seems to have been a general sense of decline. On 6
September 1566 a force of about one thousand foot soldiers and fifty
mounted troops, under the command of Colonel Edward Randolph,
set sail from Bristol. They headed up the Irish Sea, around the northern coast of Ireland and entered Lough Foyle, travelling deep into the
interior of the Ulster countryside. The fleet was one half of a great

pincer movement, the other part of which consisted of a land force led by the Lord Deputy, Sir Henry Sidney, which had set out to reduce the leader of Gaelic Ulster, the rebellious Shane O'Neill, to obedience to the Crown.

Randolph's fleet landed at Derry and made camp among the buildings of the ancient monastic settlement, expelling whatever few lay and clerical inhabitants were still living there. Derry lay on the borders of O'Neill's territory and appeared to provide a suitable base from which the English could harass the great Irish chieftain. Randolph also hoped to exploit the ancient rivalry between the O'Neills and their enemies, the O'Donnells. Calbhach, the O'Donnell chieftain, promised to support the English but, in the event, was slow to deliver on that promise. The English built earthen defence works and fortified the stone buildings of the settlement including, apparently, the Tempull Mór (cathedral) which they requisitioned as their ammunition magazine. The early seventeenth-century Catholic apologist Philip O'Sullivan Beare, said of the English that 'they performed the heretical rites of Luther, Calvin and others of that class of impious men. They left nothing undefiled by their wickedness [but] St Columba did not long delay the punishment of this sin'.

Before long, Randolph's men, unused to the damp weather in the north-west of Ireland, began to succumb to a variety of illnesses. The force was fairly quickly reduced to about seven hundred men. To add to their woes, Shane O'Neill moved his men closer to Derry, harassing the English garrison from a distance. On 15 November 1566, Randolph led his men, together with some of the local O'Dohertys who had joined him, out to face O'Neill. O'Neill was put to flight by the better-armed and better-disciplined English, having lost four hundred of his supporters. There were few casualties on the English side but among them was Colonel Randolph, who was killed.

Destruction

The English at Derry continued to harass O'Neill despite their depleted state and debilitating illnesses. By February 1567, of the surviving six hundred English troops only two hundred were able-bodied. But other Gaelic aristocrats and local people were gradually coming over to their side and were 'received to mercy' as the contemporary phrase had it. In April an accident occurred which was to change the entire situation. A fire broke out in the camp and quickly spread to all the buildings. The ammunition store caught fire and there was a huge explosion; at least thirty people were killed. It appears that an accident in a blacksmith's forge was the reason for the fire. Although Philip O'Sullivan Beare, writing some time later, argued that as a retributive miracle a wolf 'emitting from his mouth a great number of sparks, such as fly from a red hot iron when it is struck' entered the camp and set fire to the gunpowder. He adds, 'I will not take upon myself to vouch for the truth of this story; upon fame and long-standing tradition let it rest'. He also notes that as the surviving English fled from the carnage they cried out: 'The Irish *god* Columba killed us all'.

Derry was destroyed. When Queen Elizabeth I heard the news in London, 'perceiving it to come by God's ordinance, [she] beareth it well'. The garrison was withdrawn. The first attempt by the English to capture Derry was at an end. (Despite various plans throughout the sixteenth century for the return of the troops, it was not until 1600 that the English eventually returned.) Derry was devastated by the explosion and fire but some life did continue there. A certificate of ordination to the priesthood of a Patrick Mac Entagart survives, dated Pentecost Sunday, 10 June 1590. The ceremony took place in 'the cathedral church of Derry' but it is not clear which building is being referred to as the settlement had been destroyed twenty-three years earlier. In 1594 Red Hugh O'Donnell welcomed to Derry and entertained a huge force of Scots from the Western Isles who had come over to help their Gaelic 'cousins' oppose the expansion of English power in Ulster. The Nine Years' War, which was, in effect, the last-ditch stand of Gaelic Ireland against the English, had begun. The outcome would irrevocably alter the fate of Derry.

The English return

In the year 1600 another attempt was made by the English to take control of Derry. Queen Elizabeth herself seems to have been anxious to see a garrison sent there. At length, in an operation very similar to the pincer movement used against Shane O'Neill in 1566, a land force under Lord Deputy Charles Blount, VIII Baron Mountjoy, made an assault on the south-eastern borders of Ulster while, simultane-ously, a large force under the command of Sir Henry Docwra came around the coast by sea. The English entered Lough Foyle on 14 May 1600. There were four thousand foot soldiers and two hundred mounted troops in the expedition. At first, the ships became stuck in the estuarine mud which is almost invisible below the waterline on the eastern side of the lough during full tide. It took two days before they could be freed and were able to land at Culmore – the point where the river Foyle enters the lough. The new arrivals were met with sustained fire from a party of about one hundred Irishmen on the shore, but eventually the latter retired. Docwra was able to estab-lish a camp at Culmore and also at Elaghmore, a small Irish castle some miles away, where about one hundred and fifty English soldiers were stationed.

On 22 May, having left six hundred men at Culmore, the remainder of the force set out for Derry, 'a place in manner of an island ... the river called Lough Foyle encompassing it all on one side, and a bog most commonly wet and not easily passable except in two or three places, dividing it from the main land'. Docwra would not be the last English military officer to find that the Bogside of Derry was 'not easily passable'. There was no resistance to the soldiers and they quickly possessed the hill of Derry and its ruined churches, monas-teries and 'old castle'. The scene at Derry as Docwra approached must have looked much like what we would find now as we approach the ancient Irish monastic centres at places such as Clonmacnois in County Offaly and Devenish in County Fermanagh. Far from being the thriving proto-urban settlement that was described earlier in the Middle Ages, Docwra tells us that most of the hill, or 'island' of Derry as he called it, was sown with corn.

The English built their main camp out of the surviving ruins and from any supplies of timber they could get. The timber and the cockle shells they needed to collect in order to make mortar were obtained at a price – Irish snipers made it difficult for scouting par-ties to leave the base. Our very first sketch maps of Derry date to this period, sent back in dispatches to London as illustrations of the writ-ten reports also being made. The maps show us that Docwra was able to reuse some of the medieval buildings on the hillside, which he refurbished and fortified. An Irish source tells us that 'they showed neither honour nor respect to the great Saint [Colmcille], for they destroyed all the ecclesiastical edifices in the place, and made rooms and sleeping apartments of them, and used some of them to eat in'.

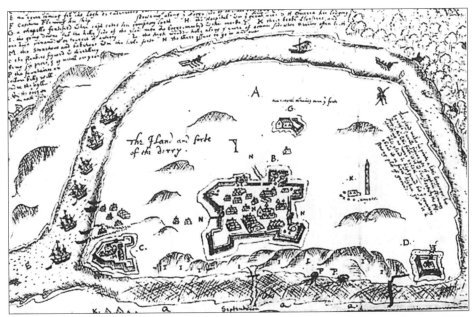

First map of Derry, 1600.

Docwra set up a string of smaller fortifications along the river and on the approaches to Derry. Like the expedition of 1566, several of the native Irish aristocrats came over to his side, including the young Cahir O'Doherty who had become leader of his people in neighbouring Inishowen in 1601 with the approval of the Crown government in Dublin. However, despite being a Gaelic chieftain in the old sense, Cahir was really no more than Docwra's puppet at this stage. He seems to have spent at least some time living inside the English camp at Derry. By all accounts he was treated very well there but, in reality, he was probably being 'detained' in 'open prison' conditions. However, having behaved particularly bravely on one occasion when he accompanied Docwra in an expedition against the O'Neills, he was recommended for a knighthood and thus became Sir Cahir O'Doherty.

The 'city of Derrie'

Like the earlier 1566 expedition, sickness began to take its toll on the English troops, but the garrison survived until the war came to an end in 1603 with victory for the Crown. The complement at Derry was reduced then, but by that stage a group of merchants and others involved with provisioning the troops had taken up residence in the settlement. Sir Henry Docwra remained on as governor. On 11 July 1604 King James I issued a charter creating a new 'city of Derrie':

> The town or borough of Derrie is, by reason of the natural seat and situation thereof, a place very convenient to be made both a town of war and a town of merchandize ... the king did ... give, grant, and confirm ... for ever a free, entire, and perfect city and county of itself, to be called the city and county of Derrie ... Sir Henry [Docwra] to be provost for life, as fully as the lord mayor of London.

The 'infant city' began to grow. George Montgomery, formerly Dean of Norwich, was appointed Protestant bishop in June 1605. He was eagerly awaited by the settlers in Derry. The Irish attorney general, Sir John Davies, hoped that Bishop Montgomery 'would come and be a new St Patrick among them'. The following year Docwra, who was disappointed by the lack of government support for the growth of the city, left Derry, selling his interests there to George Paulett who took over as commander of the garrison and vice- or acting-provost of the town. By all accounts Docwra had been a fair-minded man who was widely respected among the English and the local Gaelic population alike, but Paulett was of a different kind. The Lord Deputy believed that he was hated by those he commanded and 'neither beloved nor feared by the Irish'. He soon fell out with Sir Cahir O'Doherty who had been very close to Docwra.

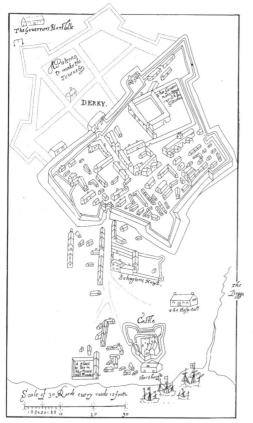

Plan for Derry, 1603.

O'Doherty's rebellion

There is still some uncertainty as to how O'Doherty came to the decision to rebel, but on 18 April 1608 he rose up against Paulett. He and his followers surprised the sleeping 'city' at 2.00am on the morning of 19 April and by dawn had captured it. The buildings of the town were destroyed and many of its citizens were taken captive. Sir Arthur Chichester, the Lord Deputy, was furious with O'Doherty: 'one so obliged to the king ... himself a burgess of the Derrie'. In the sort of outburst which we've heard repeated by English administrators in Ireland on several occasions down through the centuries (including several times during the recent Troubles), Sir Arthur castigated the Irish as 'a people that are more dangerous in peace than in war'.

O'Doherty was pursued and eventually captured and executed. His rebellion had been a total failure. Once again, and not for the last time in its history, Derry was destroyed. When it was reconstructed it would not only have new buildings but also a new name.

Colonisation and plantation

Derry did not become Londonderry until 29 March 1613 but the process by which this came about had started as early as May 1609. The previous summer (1608), a survey had been carried out in the six so called 'escheated' counties of Armagh, Cavan, Coleraine (later Derry or Londonderry), Donegal, Fermanagh and Tyrone. These were the lands deemed to be forfeit to the Crown by the so-called 'flight of the earls' – the departure or escape to the continent of the defeated leaders of Gaelic Ulster. Cahir O'Doherty's rebellion had come shortly afterwards so his lands, likewise, were confiscated by the government. The bold new plan to deal with all this land, and simultaneously to solve the contemporary version of the 'Ulster question', was 'plantation' or colonisation; the same policy was being used to exploit the land and resources of the New World in the Americas. Large numbers of 'loyal' (mainly Protestant) English and Scottish settlers would be introduced to Ulster to farm the land and secure it for Crown interests.

The wealthy merchants of the City of London (organised as trade and craft 'companies'), were coaxed into organising and sponsoring one of the plantation areas. The territory in question was based on the existing county of Coleraine with a few smaller areas added, including a strip on the west bank of the Foyle based on the ancient settlement of Derry. The Londoners were 'persuaded' that among the advantages to their becoming involved would be that:

> **Many thousands [of their unemployed citizens] would be set at work, to the great service of the King, the strength of his realm, and the advancement of several trades. It might ease [London] of an unsupportable burthen of persons ... and it would be a means to free and preserve [that] city from infection ...**

King James himself seems to have been particularly enthusiastic for the project: 'an action which is likely to prove pleasing to Almighty God, honourable to the City [of London] and profitable to the undertakers'.

There was little enthusiasm among Londoners for this enterprise in, what must have seemed to them, a land as wild and remote

'four wise, grave and discreet citizens'.

as Virginia on the other side of the Atlantic. However, the court of aldermen of the city agreed to send 'four wise, grave and discreet citizens' to Ireland to investigate conditions and possibilities. The privy council, acting for the king, wrote to Lord Deputy Chichester in Dublin explaining the importance of securing the involvement of the Londoners, emphasising that their agents would, therefore, have to be suitably impressed. It was essential that, 'matters of distaste, as fear of the Irish, of the soldiers ... and such like, be not so much as named'. Many Northern Ireland tourism and industrial development officials of recent years have been faced with similar problems and, no doubt, received similar instructions on many occasions.

The four inspectors arrived in Ulster on 22 August 1609. They spent a month touring the territory intended for them, assessing local resources and collecting and sending back to London local produce. When they got home they reported favourably on what they had seen. Immediately, the plantation began to be organised and investment money called in from the separate companies. Negotiations were opened between the City and the privy council, representing the Crown, on the details of the arrangements. The original idea was that the City of London would become a sort of 'foster mother' rather than a 'beneficial owner' of the new city of Londonderry. However, so anxious was the Crown to secure the involvement of the Londoners that all the demands of the latter were conceded. A new body, known as The Honourable The Irish Society, was set up to direct the plantation scheme. It was, in effect, a subordinate standing committee of the Corporation of London but, like many similar joint-stock companies of the time, it was set up to exploit the colonial settlement it spawned for commercial gain. That body still exists and retains interests in the Derry area but is now principally concerned with using the funds it generates for philanthropic undertakings.

The city of Londonderry

In 1610 about one hundred and thirty stonemasons and carpenters were sent over from London to begin the process of building the new city. It was an extraordinary undertaking. Most of what had survived from the medieval period and from Docwra's city was in ruins. Apparently, only two of these structures would survive into the new city: the church of the ancient Augustinian monastery and the old O'Donnell tower-house castle. Whatever houses still remained, only those required for the workers were to be retained; the rest were to be demolished. The new city was to be built on what was, effectively, a green-field site. It was to be the first planned city or town in Ireland. A drawing dated 1611 survives, showing what layout was intended at that stage. The city as actually built, however, was a slightly modified version of that plan, the layout of which, with only a few minor changes, has survived to the present day. In that sense Londonderry can be said to stand at the forefront of the history of Irish town planning.

Town planning had, of course, been revitalised during the

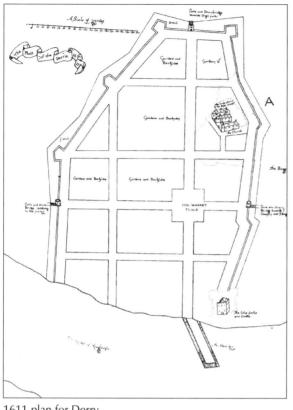

1611 plan for Derry.

Renaissance, drawing on ideas derived from the classical world. New towns, designed in imitation of the geometric layout of Roman military camps, were being built all over Europe. Londonderry bears a striking resemblance in layout (although not in topography), to the frontier city of Vitry-le-François in eastern France. Vitry had been finished in 1560 for Francis II, King of France, who was married to Mary Queen of Scots, mother of James I who was the progenitor of Londonderry. It is possible that this family connection may have influenced the design of the new city in Ulster. Vitry was built on the river Marne in a similar manner to the way in which Londonderry was built on the river Foyle. There are differences between the plans of the two cities but these can be explained by local topographical circumstances.

It took many years for the houses to be erected along the streets and for the public buildings of the town to be completed. The walls and gates were not finished until 1618 and it was another ten years before the main church of the settlement, St Columb's Cathedral, was even begun. Gradually the city also filled up with people as settlers moved to Derry from England and Scotland. In 1615, while construction work was still ongoing, a clumsy conspiracy by some of the native Irish to rebel and burn all the colonial settlements was uncovered. The perpetrators were arrested and brought to trial. The hearing, which was held amidst the confusion of the half-built city, interestingly included two native Irishmen on the jury. Seventeen defendants – all of them men – were put on trial. Eleven were released but six were found guilty and sentenced to be drawn 'in chains to the gallows where they would be hanged but when only half dead to be cut down, disembowelled, beheaded, the body quartered and then burned'. Following the executions of these men, their heads were to be exhibited on the city gates. Earlier this century there was an attempt to submit the names of these six men to the Sacred Congregation of Rites in Rome as candidates for the title of Martyr of the Roman Catholic Church. However, the matter was not pursued.

The first 'siege'

It was not until the outbreak of the general native uprising in Ulster in October 1641 that the city experienced another such threat. The rebels, led by Sir Phelim O'Neill, quickly took control of most of Ulster but no attempt was made to attack Derry. Instead, the city became a centre of refuge for the settlers fleeing before the insurgents. Many of these 'refugees' continued their journey onwards to Scotland, leaving from the port of Derry. The city was vastly

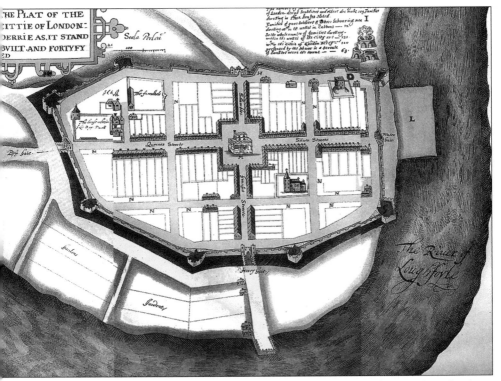

The city of Londonderry.

overcrowded and starvation quickly took hold. The citizens prepared whatever defences they could. Among the measures they took was to order some of the native Irish who lived there to leave the city. They agreed:

> to expell all such Irish out of the city, as we shall conceive to be needful for the safety of this city ... That after this is done ... a proclamation be made, that no man or woman so expelled the city shall, upon pain of death, return ... or make their abode within two miles of the same.

The situation in Ireland became even more confused as a result of the contemporary political struggles in Britain between King Charles I, the English Parliament and the Scots. Various sections of the population in Ireland sided with different factions in Britain. To make matters even more complicated it was at this time that Presbyterianism was first introduced formally to Ulster. This was achieved by the vanguard of Scottish soldiers who came over to assist the colonists against the native rebels. The political and religious establishment in Londonderry, led by the Anglican bishop and the Mayor, was solidly opposed to Presbyterianism. This led the establishment into serious dispute with its citizens, the majority of whom supported the Presbyterian cause.

The situation in both islands continued to deteriorate and to grow more complex throughout the 1640s, particularly after the execution of Charles I in January 1649. Londonderry at that time was garrisoned by troops loyal to the English Parliament but the vast majority of the settlers were disgusted by the king's execution. As a result, the extraordinary and unexpected occurred in March when the city was besieged by local Presbyterian 'royalist' forces. Even more extraordinary was the eventual end of the siege on 8 August 1649 when native Catholic forces, led by Owen Roe O'Neill, drove off the besiegers and entered the city to relieve the parliamentary garrison. A contemporary noted that the Presbyterians 'did not expect to see the [Irish] Roman Catholic party leagued with the [English] republicans in opposing the royalists'. One might add that these events are not at all what the current descendants of any of these parties might expect to find in their history.

One week after the end of the first 'siege of Derry', Oliver

Cromwell landed in Ireland and the whole country came under the control of his 'republicans'. Cromwell's mission, as one historian has put it, included 'not only conquest but also revenge'. The infamous slaughter he visited on the people of Drogheda and Wexford was not repeated in the north-west of the country, but the native Irish were defeated by Cromwell's supporters in the battle of Scarrifhollus, near Letterkenny in County Donegal, in 1650. Some sporadic fighting continued in Ulster for another few years but the end result was that the few Catholic or native Irish who had managed to hold on to their land until then, now lost it.

Catholic control under James II

The city of Derry gradually recovered from the upheaval and remained calm for another forty years or so until the next great crisis in its history, also sparked off by events in London. When the Protestant king, Charles II, died in 1685 he was replaced by his brother, James II, a devout convert to Catholicism. James appointed Richard Talbot, the Earl of Tyrconnell, as his Lord Deputy in Ireland (the

Londonderry, c. 1685.

effective governor of the country). Tyrconnell set about changing the previously all-Protestant establishment of the country, placing Catholics in high office in the army and in prominent local government positions. In Derry, a Catholic, Cormick O'Neill from Broughshane in County Antrim, was appointed Mayor and the formerly all-Protestant corporation was reorganised. This new corporation consisted of the Mayor, twenty aldermen and forty burgesses. Its religious or ethnic make-up can be discerned from the words of the somewhat partisan, mid-nineteenth-century local historian, Robert Simpson: 'Of this corporation there were twenty-eight *great O's* and six *Macs*'.

Tyrconnell then withdrew the Protestant garrison from the almost totally Protestant city of Londonderry and the citizens grew anxious and fearful for their lives and fortunes. On 7 December 1688, amid growing rumours and a deepening political crisis in Ireland and Britain, a group of thirteen so-called 'resolute apprentice boys' shut the city gates, preventing the admission of a contingent of Catholic soldiers who had arrived to garrison the city. As the Reverend George Walker wrote later:

> A great number of the younger, and some of the meaner sort of the inhabitants ran happily to the gates and shut them, loudly denying entrance to such *guests*, and obstinately refusing obedience to us. At first we were amazed at the enterprise, and apprehensive of the many ill circumstances and consequences, that might result from so rash an undertaking; but since that ... we began to consider it as an especial instance of God's mercy towards us, that we were not delivered over as prey unto them and that it pleased him to stir up the spirits of the people so unexpectedly to provide for their and our common safety, and preservation.

The interesting parallels between this event and the actions of some of Derry's Catholic youths in the late 1960s – when they built barricades and established the so-called 'Free Derry' in the Bogside area preventing the admission of the 'Protestant' security forces – has not gone totally unnoticed.

'Williamite' Derry

Eventually, after some negotiation over the following weeks, just before the end of 1688 a Protestant garrison under the command of Robert Lundy was admitted to the city. By that stage events in England had outstripped those in Ireland. The 'Glorious Revolution' had taken place. James II had fled his throne and taken refuge in the court of Louis XIV in France. William of Orange had come from The Netherlands to England – ironically, before crossing to England the defence of the Dutch 'Republic' against the ambitions of Louis XIV had been William's greatest concern. In February 1689 William and his wife, Mary, daughter of King James, were crowned king and queen in London. However, William, as well as being James's son-in-law, was also his nephew; he was a son of James's sister and, therefore, was also cousin to his wife. This family 'difficulty' and the events which gave rise to it and flowed from it are arguably still being played out in Northern Ireland and on the streets of Derry. Catholic Ireland flocked to the cause of King James while Protestant Ireland, and in particular Protestant Ulster, joined the cause of King 'Billy'. Londonderry was to be one of the principal stages where the two sides would meet in confrontation.

Derry now became a refuge and a symbol of Protestant support for King William. Thousands of settlers from all over Ulster gathered inside its protective walls. Some estimates (probably exaggerated) suggest that the population of the city rose from about two thousand to about thirty thousand. It is difficult to imagine how so many people could be accommodated inside a space which is no more than five hundred yards long by three hundred yards wide at its broadest part. Nevertheless, whatever the truth, the city was put under immense strain. The situation got so bad that some of the city's leaders, in particular Robert Lundy, cautioned that they could not hold out. Lundy came under grave suspicion of being a traitor and was eventually persuaded that, for his own safety, he should leave the city. Tried and condemned

Effigy of Robert Lundy, the traitor, in the Tower Museum.

by the court of public opinion and one-sided history, his name has been synonymous with treachery ever since. 'Lundy' is still an abusive term favoured by sections of the Protestant or loyalist population in Northern Ireland. Was Lundy a traitor? Paradoxically, if he was, it was not to the Protestant or Williamite cause as was and is claimed, but to the cause of the Catholic King James from whom he had originally accepted his military commission!

James II in Ireland

In the meantime, James II had come to Ireland to use it as a base for regaining the English throne. With a mixed force of some loyal British soldiers and Irish and French troops he made his way north to obtain the submission of the rebellious city of Derry. This, it was argued, would be essential before he could cross to Scotland, eventually to make his way south to London. Along with the professional soldiers based in the city, Derry had organised a citizens' garrison. When James himself appeared before the city on the morning of 18 April, amid the shouts of what would become the famous Ulster slogan of 'No Surrender', some of the more highly spirited and less disciplined defenders actually fired on the king and his entourage. This was outright revolution. Some of the less radical individuals inside the walls sent an apology to the king. Although it is unlikely that everyone will be happy to accept it, it has to be said that, despite what has happened in Derry over the past thirty years or so, there can have been few more truly 'republican' acts carried out in its long history than this actual attack on the person of James, king according to the doctrine of Divine Right. James himself was not hurt but some in his party were killed. The demoralised and disconsolate king remained sitting on his horse all day, in the rain, waiting unsuccessfully for a surrender. When this did not happen he withdrew and gave orders for the 'siege' to begin in earnest.

The Siege of Derry

It has often been argued, on the basis of military technicalities, that the 'Siege of Derry' was not in fact a siege. No real attempt was made to storm the city walls although there were a few hand-to-hand skirmishes. The 'besiegers', positioned on the hills all around the city, were badly armed and equipped. For the most part they relied on their blockade to starve those inside the city into surrender. Most of those who died during the siege did so from hunger and disease, although the besiegers did fire mortar bombs high into the air which fell onto the roofs of houses, injuring and killing some of the

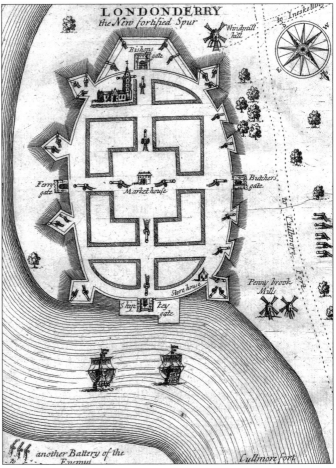

The Siege of Derry.

occupants. James had given orders for humanitarian conduct during the campaign, but at the beginning of June a Lithuanian named Conrad de Rosen, who was a Marshal General in the French army, arrived in support of James and began to operate a much tougher policy.

The Reverend George Walker, who at the time was a governor inside the city, described Rosen in Cromwellian terms and said that he

> 'swore by the belly of God, he would demolish our town and bury us in its ashes putting all to the sword, without consideration of age or sex and would study the most exquisite torments to lengthen the misery and pain of all he found obstinate, or active in opposing his commands and pleasure.'

Shortly before Rosen's arrival the French Chief of Artillery, Jean-Bernard Desjeans, Sieur de Pointis, had constructed a 'boom' or floating barricade across the river Foyle (just to the north of the location of the present Foyle Bridge), to prevent any relief ships reaching Derry.

Some ships did arrive from England in the second week of June but they did not attempt to get past the boom. Instead, they withdrew and sailed around the coast into nearby Lough Swilly where, in a somewhat unorthodox fashion, communications were established with those inside the beleaguered city. The 'inscrutable heroe' who carried messages to and from the city was, according to Governor Walker's coy words,

> 'a little boy that with great ingenuity made two dispatches ... [One] made up within a piece of a bladder, in the shape of a suppositor, and the same way applied to the boy ...'

If it isn't too irreverent to say so, one could suggest that this lad was not the only Derry child to have had the consequences of the city's history 'applied' to his anatomy in this way, at least if one is speaking metaphorically. Indeed, a statue to this anonymous little boy might one day rival the fame of the Mannekin Pis in Brussels!

Conditions inside the city during the siege were atrocious but by all accounts they were not much better for the besiegers outside the walls. The weather was appalling that summer and this, of course, only added to the universal misery. Towards the end of July the relief ships in Lough Swilly were ordered to return to Lough Foyle to try to break through the boom. On the evening of 28 July an attempt was launched. Amid gunfire from the shore those on board a small boat, the *Swallow,* which preceded the ships, attacked the boom with axes to weaken it. The *Mountjoy,* a local Derry ship, followed, crashing into the boom. After a number of mishaps the barrier was breached and the relief ships sailed upriver to the stricken city. There were tremendous celebrations despite the fact that the besieging Jacobites kept firing at the city. However, after 105 days the siege had effectively been ended. Three days later the besieging troops conceded defeat and moved away from Derry.

Consequences of the Siege

The War of the Two Kings moved elsewhere and included, in the following year (1690), the famous Battle of the Boyne in County Meath.
Derry was left in peace to reconstruct the broken lives of its citizens
as well as their shattered buildings. Various consequences and controversies followed the siege. Presbyterians felt that they had not got
due credit for the role played in the defence of the city by their co-
religionists. A war of words, in the form of published pamphlets, followed quickly as differing interpretations of the events were written
by Anglican and Presbyterian apologists respectively. For a long time
afterwards many of the citizens felt that they had been cheated by an
ungrateful government in London of the necessary compensation for
the losses they had sustained. Almost as soon as the siege was over
the process of mythologising its significance began. The story of the
siege became the subject of a large number of literary and artistic
works which ranged from the relatively serious and critical to the
wildly imaginative and propagandistic.

Since the late nineteenth century in particular, the terminol-
ogy and events of the siege have provided a vocabulary and a parable
for describing the political situation of the Ulster Protestant population. It is the practice of Protestant and unionist writers and speak-
ers to praise the siege and the associated events of the war for the
role played by their ancestors in the defence of all 'religious and civil
liberties'. Such an argument is indefensible in the light of the Penal
Laws against Catholics and Presbyterians which were enacted shortly
after the end of the siege. Far from ushering in such liberties for all,
the Penal Laws introduced a form of apartheid which took a long
time to remove; it has taken an even longer time to remove their
influence. Notwithstanding this, the Siege of Derry was a very significant event in the history of the city and provided many examples of
courage and humanitarianism on both sides, as well as acts of human
folly. Stripped of sectarian triumphalism, it is absolutely right that it
should be commemorated and even celebrated. All sections of the
community have lessons to learn, and a few surprises to learn about,
in the story of the siege.

Disappointment with how they were treated by the Penal Laws in the aftermath of the siege and the War of the Two Kings led some Presbyterians to leave Ulster and head for a better life in North America. Among the first of these transatlantic emigrants was a party led by Reverend James McGregor of Aghadowey in County Derry. Reverend McGregor had fought in the siege. He took most of his congregation with him, comparing their departure, on the eve of their journey, with the story of Moses leading the chosen tribes to the promised land. They arrived in Boston early in August 1718 and eventually settled in what became the towns of Derry and Londonderry in the state of New Hampshire. Several other shiploads of emigrants left for America from the port of Derry that summer, beginning a tradition of emigration which lasted until the twentieth century.

Most, but not all, of the eighteenth-century emigrants came from the Ulster Presbyterian community. They would become known in America as the Ulster Scots. Paradoxically, they brought with them a tradition of 'republicanism', a fact which might disturb some of the present-day descendants of their co-religionists who stayed behind in Ireland. The Ulster Scots played an extremely important role in the struggle for American independence and provided the new republic with many of its early presidents, as well as other leaders. Historians still debate whether it was essentially religious discrimination or economic depression which caused them to leave – no doubt it was a mixture of both.

During the eighteenth century Derry was probably the premier Irish port for transatlantic emigration. The emigrating ships landed at many different American ports but most particularly at Philadelphia. Most of the ships used in Derry were owned by local businessmen and the 'emigration trade' became a major element in the city's economy, as it continued to be in the nineteenth century. An advertisement for the ship *Hopewell*, set to leave from Derry in the summer of 1766, gives a flavour of what the emigrants hoped to gain by their departure:

> 'It would swell the advertisement to too great a length
> to enumerate all the blessings those people enjoy who
> have already removed from this country to said province. It may suffice to say, that from tenants they are

become landlords, from working for others they now work for themselves, and enjoy the fruits of their own industry.'

The quays of Derry in the early twentieth century.

However, many of the emigrants had to finance their passage by signing on as indentured servants, thereby mortgaging their future work and earnings.

Eighteenth-century Derry

In 1706 the population of the city was estimated at 2,850 persons. By the end of the eighteenth century it had risen to about eleven thousand. The overwhelming majority of the residents were Protestants. This was a colonial – indeed an 'apartheid' – society, governed either directly or indirectly by the Penal Laws which placed Catholics, and to a lesser extent non-conforming (ie, non-Anglican) Protestants, under severe legal pressures and discriminations. However, as the century progressed, one by one these laws were either removed or abandoned.

A Catholic ghetto had formed outside the city walls in the area which would later become known as the Bogside. In 1784 the first Catholic chapel built in Derry since the plantation was opened on or close to the site of a medieval church. Although considerably enlarged and refurbished on several occasions since then, that church, the 'Long Tower', still survives as a much-loved building. Contributions to the building fund came from the all-Protestant corporation and from the Anglican bishop, Frederick Augustus Hervey. Hervey, as well as being (Protestant) Bishop of Derry, was also the Earl of Bristol. He was a leading public figure of his day, an eccentric man and, by all accounts, totally devoid of sectarianism. It was probably Hervey who set the tone of enlightenment and ecumenism which seems to have permeated the life of Derry at that time, especially in the 1780s. One of the most interesting displays

Eighteenth-century Derry.

of this positive mood was evident in the celebrations of 1788 and 1789, the centenary years of the Siege of Derry. The Catholic community took part in these events with their principal clergy actually walking in the main parades. Change was in the air. It was probably not entirely coincidental that the summer of 1789 also saw the outbreak of the French Revolution.

The *Londonderry Journal* for 17 August 1789 reported:

'Last Thursday ... the Londonderry Independent Volunteers, commanded by Captain John Ferguson, fired three volleys in the Diamond, in commemoration of the Relief of Derry, 1689. Captain Ferguson entertained the company at dinner, where the following, among other toasts, were given:- "The Glorious Revolution of 1688;" "The Army;" "The Fleet;" "Perpetual unanimity between Great Britain and Ireland;" "The Whig Club of Ireland;" "The President of the United

States;" "The French Revolutionists and Liberty to all Mankind".'

This atmosphere did not last for long. Ten years later, during the rebellion of 1798, Derry was strongly loyal to the government and in 1801 the city supported the Act of Union with Britain.

The 'picturesque' town

Bishop Hervey was not only an ideal churchman, he was also a well-known art collector, traveller and builder. The ruins of his great house at Downhill, twenty miles north of Derry, can be visited and some of his other building works are still to be found in Derry itself. He made many practical contributions to his diocese and its inhabitants of all religions. Perhaps his most influential gift to the city was

the first bridge across the river Foyle – a cause which he championed. Prior to its construction in 1790–91, the only way to cross the river was by ferry. Cynics remarked that the bishop's interest was primarily personal as, due to his frequent travels away from Derry, he was likely to be one of the bridge's most frequent users.

The 'earl bishop'.

There are many images and descriptions of Derry during the eighteenth century. Most, if not all, of these stress its picturesqueness. The great Irish philosopher, George Berkeley, was appointed to the prestigious and lucrative post of Dean of Derry in 1724. He held the post until 1732, although largely as an absentee. When he visited the city on first being appointed he was favourably impressed.

> 'I have hardly seen a more agreeable situation, the town standing on a peninsula in the midst of a fine spreading lake, environed with green hills, and at a

> distance the noble ridge of Inishowen and the mighty
> rocks of Magilligan form a most august scene.'

The traveller Arthur Young, who visited Derry in the 1770s during his tour of Ireland, said of the city that it was 'the most picturesque of any place I have seen'. Despite all the vicissitudes since then, particularly in the past thirty years, the city still retains much of what these and other eighteenth-century writers praised, including some of its fine Georgian frontages.

Nineteenth-century expansion

In the early nineteenth century the city began to expand beyond the limits imposed by its seventeenth-century walls. The new bridge had facilitated the development of a 'middle class' suburb in the Waterside and gradually, as the century progressed, other public institutions and buildings were set up there. In addition, the city began to expand on its northern side, again with public institutions of various kinds and middle class houses. A Protestant working or lower class area began to develop in the Wapping district on the south side of the walled city in parallel to the similar Catholic district of the Bogside. Conditions in these areas were fairly bad and disease and high mortality were the common lot of the inhabitants. Despite this poverty, however, Catholics from the neighbouring country districts, in particular from County Donegal, began to arrive into the city in large numbers. In 1814 the population of the city was estimated at 14,000 persons. By 1834 this had risen to almost 19,000, of whom just over half were Catholics. By the time of the 1851 census, Catholics were a clear but largely unenfranchised majority in the city. It would take until the outbreak of the Troubles and the local government reforms of 1973, however, to translate this majority into actual municipal power.

The increase in the number of Catholics living in the city as the nineteenth century progressed was unprecedented and unexpected. Sectarian tension and conflict began to grow as a result, often focused on the siege anniversary parades now held annually. The Apprentice Boys organisation – established in Derry in 1814 – had grown out of hostility to the contemporary campaign being waged by Daniel O'Connell seeking Catholic Emancipation. This was a

Early nineteenth-century Derry.

movement which sought the removal of restrictions on Catholics in Britain and Ireland which prevented them from holding various government and legal offices and, most importantly, from sitting in Parliament.

The emancipation crisis also led to another development in the city. The *Londonderry Journal* (now the *Derry Journal* and Ireland's second oldest newspaper) had been founded in 1772 as a liberal Protestant voice. It subsequently adopted a more conservative outlook, but in 1829 its new owners changed editorial policy again to welcome Catholic Emancipation. The editor vehemently disagreed and left to found his own newspaper, the *Londonderry Sentinel*. That newspaper still survives as the organ of local Protestant opinion.

Many of the Catholics who moved into Derry at this time found work as labourers in the building boom which was taking place as the city expanded. Around 1830 a local businessman, William Scott, began the shirt-making industry which was to develop rapidly and become one of the economic mainstays of the city. The industry had grown out of the older linen-working practice and the tradition among local women of 'sprigging' (white embroidery on a white background). It was not, however, until the 1850s, with the arrival of the portable sewing machine and the introduction of the factory system, that the industry really took off. In the second half of the nineteenth century shirt-factory buildings sprang up all over the city and in neighbouring villages and towns. The industry continued to be a mixture of the 'factory system' and a 'cottage' or home-based craft, a fact which was noted by Karl Marx in his seminal work, *Das Kapital*. Another of the peculiarities of the industry was the predominance of women in the workforce. Ninety percent of the workers were women, giving to the factories, and to the social life of the city itself, a distinctive character. The industry reached its peak in the 1920s, by then employing about 18,000 people.

Shipping and emigration

Shipping and the emigration trade continued to contribute to the local economy. Some shipbuilding was continued in the city but the industry never developed on the scale of that in Belfast. One of the city's notable entrepreneurs was Captain William Coppin who, in 1843, launched his *Great Northern*, the largest screw propulsion vessel of its kind yet built anywhere in the world. However, notwithstanding the technical brilliance of the ship, Coppin failed to capitalise on his success.

'Derry Kay' [quay], as the point of embarkation for many who set sail for the New World, entered the imagination of thousands of people on both sides of the Atlantic and was commemorated in hundreds of ballads and stories. At first, American trading vessels carried passengers across the Atlantic, having previously arrived in Derry with consignments of flaxseed for the Ulster linen industry. By about 1815 some of the Derry merchants began to enter the trade themselves having purchased small, Canadian-built sailing vessels of up to three hundred tonnes. Emigrants were carried on the outward journey and then the ships picked up cargoes of timber and cotton for the return voyage.

By the 1840s these smaller vessels had disappeared to be replaced by a Derry-owned fleet of larger ships. The need for bigger ships meant that fewer merchants were involved and eventually the business passed into the hands of just two local companies: J. & J.L. Cooke and William McCorkell & Company. Many of the ships in the McCorkell fleet were named after characters in Henry Wadsworth Longfellow's poem, *The Song of Hiawatha*, including one of the best-loved Derry ships, the *Minnehaha*. During the American Civil War, however, steamships were introduced onto the Atlantic crossing. The Derry sailing vessels became increasingly marginalised and, although they held on until the 1890s by diversifying and sailing to the less-developed ports on the east and west coasts of South America (and even occasionally up to San Francisco), they were inevitably put out of business.

Shipquay St, mid-nineteenth century.

Most of the nineteenth-century emigrants, particularly after the Great Famine of the 1840s, were Catholics. The Famine reaped its grim effects on the countryside in the hinterland of Derry and many destitute and frightened people flocked to the city in search of relief, despite the fact that the municipal authorities made it clear that refugees were not welcome. Some of these, however, did manage to get into the recently opened workhouse, while those with some resources were able to leave on the emigrant ships.

Sectarianism

As the nineteenth century progressed sectarian difficulties continued to dog the city. In 1869, during a visit to Derry by Prince Arthur, a son of Queen Victoria, intercommunal rioting occurred leading to the deaths of three people. If one were to ignore the dates on the report of the official inquiry into these events, it could be taken as an account of what happened again in Derry exactly one hundred years later in 1969:

Both gentlemen [police officers] then went over to the crowd to persuade the Bogside party to go home. Some of them, addressing the officer said, 'Mr. Stafford, we will go home, if you will get the other parties off the [city] wall; for if we go down there we will be murdered.' There were from eighty to a hundred of this party in the Diamond, and their direct way to the Bogside lay through Butcher's Gate, which those on the wall, who were flinging stones, and it was said firing pistols also, from it, had the command of. Those on the wall were of the Apprentice Boy party.

The city walls and the Bogside, with the Walker Pillar.

Not all the differences were between Catholics and Protestants. There were tensions too between Presbyterians and members of the Church of Ireland. This situation had been evident since the earliest days of the Londonderry settlement but had taken on an added vigour in the aftermath of the siege of 1689. In 1868 a short-term alliance between Catholic and liberal Presbyterian voters managed to win the parliamentary seat for the city from the local Tory establishment. The alliance held together for several years despite the real likelihood on a number of occasions of a break along traditional denominational lines.

The arrangement came to an end in 1872 at the first election held in Ireland to be conducted using the newly-introduced secret ballot arrangements. In a complicated contest the seat was won by the Conservative candidate, Charles Lewis. Lewis was a London Presbyterian and his co-religionists deserted their former Catholic associates to vote for him. With the growth of the Home Rule movement and the increasing social confidence of Derry's Catholics, Protestant solidarity progressively became a dominant concern. An opportunity for overt expression of this point of view occurred during the muted events in 1888 and 1889 celebrating the two-hundredth anniversary of the siege. Protestant unity was by then a reality and Derry's two communities, whose combined number in 1900 was about 40,000, found themselves totally polarised.

In 1833, during Daniel O'Connell's Repeal [of the Union with Britain] campaign, Lord Macaulay, speaking in the House of Commons, had first suggested that partition might be a solution to the internal problem in Ireland. Any argument in support of Irish independence, he suggested, 'would in a tenfold degree apply in favour of one domestic legislature in Dublin, and another in Derry, or some other large town in the north of Ireland'. At the time that he spoke, Catholics probably already made up a majority of the population of Derry, but they were largely an invisible majority. By the turn of the century that invisibility had been removed but, except for the occasional electoral victory, it had not been translated into political power. An important by-election in 1913 returned a local shirt-manufacturer, David Hogg, to Parliament. Hogg was a Protestant and had not committed himself to Home Rule, but he had been the choice of the Catholic clergy whose authority in the selection of 'nationalist' candidates was, at that time, total.

1916: the Easter Rising and the Somme

As elsewhere in Ireland, the period between 1912 and the start of the First World War in 1914 saw tension rising over the Home Rule issue between nationalists and unionists in Derry. The two opposing, recently-founded paramilitary organisations, the (Protestant) Ulster Volunteer Force (UVF) and the (Catholic) Irish Volunteers, began to organise in the city. The outbreak of the war in Europe, however, led to a temporary truce as large contingents from both sides of the community divide in Derry set out for the continent as part of the British forces.

During the 1916 Easter Rising in Dublin, Derry remained totally calm. Such few local 'republicans' as existed (about nine in all), were arrested and interned. Only one person from Derry actually died in the Rising and he was serving on the Crown side: twenty-year-old Second Lieutenant Charles Crockett of the 12th Inniskilling Fusiliers was killed on Saturday, 29 April, the day the Rising ended.

Derry in the early twentieth century.

The only Derry man arrested during the chaos in Dublin was David Norrie, the local Unionist Party registration agent and General Secretary of the Apprentice Boys of Derry. Norrie had gone to Dublin to attend the opening of a new branch of his organisation. When the Rising broke out, he found himself trapped in an Orange Hall near the city centre. On emerging he was arrested and, ironically, ended up in Wakefield Prison in England along with hundreds of republican prisoners. After representations, however, he was released.

Many of Norrie's Protestant acquaintances and colleagues who had joined the British Army and gone off to the war on the continent were not so lucky. The 10th Inniskillings (known as the 'Derrys'), had been formed from the Derry UVF. At the Battle of the Somme, which started on 1 July 1916, the Derrys were the most successful section in the Ulster Division. They got as far as the fifth German line but were subsequently mowed down. Of the 764 men who went 'over the top' on that morning only 346 were able to answer the roll-call on the following day.

The impressive war memorial in the Diamond, at the centre of the old walled city, commemorates the Derry victims of both World Wars. It is by the sculptor Vernon March and was erected in 1927.

Partition

At the 1918 election, following the end of the war, Derry returned the Sinn Féin candidate Eoin MacNeill to the breakaway Dáil Éireann in Dublin. MacNeill was a distinguished cultural activist and a scholar of early Irish history. Unfortunately, the end of the war also brought an end to the economic boom which had accompanied the hostilities, especially for the Derry clothing industry. Unemployment figures began to climb steadily again and the deteriorating social conditions aided the spread of political tension and rising sectarianism. In a bid to counter the rise of Sinn Féin nationwide, the government had introduced proportional representation for the local elections of 1920. Paradoxically, in Derry this led to the appointment of the city's first Catholic mayor (apart from the short-lasting Cormick O'Neill in 1688), the nationalist, Hugh C. O'Doherty. Tension continued to build as preparations were being made by the government for the partition of Ireland. In April, May and June of that year serious rioting and gun-battles took place in the city. In all, forty people were killed. By Christmas 1920, Ireland had been effectively partitioned and, despite the total opposition of the local (majority) Catholic and nationalist community, Derry remained in the United Kingdom, part of the six counties that formed the state of Northern Ireland.

Gerrymandering

There was some opposition to the elections in May 1921 for the new Parliament of Northern Ireland and an attempt later that year by republican councillors to pass a motion of allegiance to the Dáil in Dublin. However, the signing of the Anglo-Irish Treaty and the subsequent formal acceptance by the southern state, in December 1921, of the partition of the country left nationalists in Derry with no option but to accept their new status. They hoped that their situation would be altered by the promised Boundary Commission which was to be appointed to adjust the border in accordance with the wishes of local people. The new Northern Ireland government abolished proportional representation for local-government elections and approved a manipulated rearrangement of the electoral areas which undemocratically restored the unionist advantage in the city. Despite the fact that nationalists were an overwhelming majority of the population, this 'gerrymander' ensured that unionists continued to control the corporation until its abolition in 1968.

The Boundary Commission was not established until November 1924, with prominent unionist J.R. Fisher representing Northern Ireland, a South African Supreme Court judge, Richard Feetham, as chairman and the former Derry Sinn Féin M.P. Eoin MacNeill representing the southern government. The Commission made a number of visits to Derry, including an occasion when the Mayor organised a Sunday afternoon excursion to the great prehistoric and early medieval monument, the Grianán of Aileach, on the other side of the border in County Donegal. This incident later led to the inaccurate but slanderous criticism that MacNeill, the eminent Gaelic professor, was more interested in archaeology than in the fate of the Derry nationalists.

The border

In November 1925 the chairman of the Boundary Commission, Judge Feetham, announced to his colleagues that it was his personal belief that 'economic and geographic factors' ought to take precedence over the 'wishes of the inhabitants'. This opinion was leaked to the press (almost certainly maliciously), forcing Eoin MacNeill to resign. The following year, all three governments signed an agreement abandoning the Commission and accepting the status quo. Derry remained part of Northern Ireland and of the United Kingdom, cut off by all the paraphernalia of an international border from its natural hinterland in County Donegal. The border created unprecedented barriers to local trade and commerce and even to communications. For example, one of the railway lines out of the city crossed and re-crossed the new frontier seventeen times. The railway company was responsible for paying all customs costs. Some businesses, anxious to maintain their traditional customers now in the Irish Free State, actually transferred out of the city. These measures, coming at the same time as the post-war depression and international economic decline, helped to bring about an official unemployment figure in 1926 of 28 percent. Massive emigration from the city, particularly of Catholics, began again.

One of the strangest and most humiliating features of the employment market in the city around this time was the annual Rabble Days or 'hiring fairs', held in May and December each year. This was an opportunity for local farmers to inspect and hire agricultural labourers and domestic servants. The business was conducted in the open air in the Diamond and huge crowds gathered to watch the street entertainers who also congregated there and in the surrounding streets.

The 1930s

The 1930s saw a little bit of aviation glamour in the city on two separate occasions. On 22 May 1932, Amelia Earhart landed in a field just north of the city at Ballyarnett. She had flown overnight from Harbour Grace, Newfoundland, thus becoming the first woman to fly solo across the Atlantic. She had intended to fly to Paris in imitation of Charles Lindbergh but had changed her mind, obviously attracted by the greater charms of Derry – in fact, she had run out of fuel and had to land at the first available spot. The following year the city saw more aviation excitement when it became a refuelling base for the great transatlantic Italian flying boat armada, led by General Italo Balbo. The whole exercise was a propaganda stunt for the Fascist government of Benito Mussolini, but it was given an enthusiastic welcome in Derry, especially by the small local Italian community. In the same year a new bridge across the river Foyle, the Craigavon Bridge, was built alongside its predecessor, the Carlisle Bridge, which was then demolished.

In 1936, anxious that their majority position in the corporation was coming under threat, unionist councillors implemented a new scheme for the government of the city. It reduced the number of wards or electoral districts down to three, effectively two Protestant or unionist wards with a combined population of just over 7,000 voters, and a Catholic or nationalist ward with a population of around 9,000 voters. However, as the two unionist wards together returned twelve councillors and the nationalist ward only eight, the latter found themselves in a permanent minority. One unionist councillor famously admitted that it did seem 'a bit slightly out of proportion'. By the 1938 local elections the system was in place. At the first meeting of the new corporation the leader of the nationalists, Paddy Maxwell, remarked that 'numbers will tell in the end'. The 'end', however, did not come for another thirty years.

The Second World War

Whatever the local problems and conflicts, as was the case in 1914, the outbreak of the Second World War brought about a temporary truce. In an unexpected way the war was very good to Derry. There were plenty of jobs – effectively it was the only time in modern history when there was full employment in the city. The influx of a vast number of foreign military personnel into the city, especially the glamorous Americans, lifted the city out of the depressing dullness and insularity of the 1930s. A secret agreement which had been signed between the British and the Americans in 1941, before the latter had entered the war, provided for the setting up of a United States naval base in Derry. On 30 June 1941, 362 'civilian technicians' arrived. That number was doubled before Christmas of the same year. By the time of the attack on Pearl Harbour on 7 December 1941, after which the Americans did enter the war, a huge network of US facilities had been built in Derry. These included storage depots, radio installations, a ship-repair base, a new quayside at Lisahally, as well as domestic accommodation and administration offices. Later, other facilities would also be added.

The US Naval Operating Base, Londonderry, was officially commissioned on 5 February 1942. Derry was the first US navy establishment in Europe and became the terminal for US convoys bound for Britain. The base continued in operation until July 1944 when the installation was handed over to the British, leaving only a US radio station behind; this was not closed until 1977. Many of those who came to staff the base initially were transferred from a similar US installation in Iceland. Despite its conservative tradition of

Protestant sabbatharianism, the Americans claimed that after
Reykjavik Derry 'seemed like Coney Island'.

An official American source said of the Londonderry base:

> 'Until the creation of Exeter, Londonderry was the
> main supply depot for our naval activities in the British
> Isles, and throughout the war it was the major United
> States naval radio station in the European theatre.'

Quite apart from the British forces stationed in the city, there
were nearly as many Canadians as Americans in Derry during the war.
Contingents from the 'free' forces of France, Belgium and Holland
were stationed there also.

War Memorial, the Diamond, early this century.

Northern Ireland's official war historian, Professor J. W. Blake,
claimed that from a British point of view,

> 'Londonderry held the key to victory in the Atlantic ...
> Londonderry was the most important escort base in
> the North-Western approaches.'

Four important wartime airfields were built close to the city,
one of which, at Eglinton, now serves as the City of Derry Airport.
One of the other airfields, now out of commission, is currently the
site of the giant Du Pont industrial complex at Maydown.

Spitfires and other military aircraft from these airfields were a common sight over Lough Foyle. The city's location on the border with the 'Free State', which, of course, was neutral throughout the war, was repeatedly exploited for wartime smuggling.

Damage to the city itself was limited to just one occasion. On Easter Tuesday, 15 April 1941 a single German bomber dropped two parachute mines over the river Foyle, probably intended for the busy ship-repair base below. One of the bombs fell near Pennyburn Catholic Church, which a local eyewitness (probably shell-shocked) claimed was protected from a direct hit when the statue of St Patrick on the exterior of the building 'shoved' the bomb away! Others were not so lucky: fifteen people lost their lives when the second bomb exploded as it fell on Messines Park. This was a small ex-servicemen's housing estate named after Messines in Belgium where some of the men had seen service in the First World War. Ironically, Adolf Hitler had also served as a Private on the German side at Messines. On the same night that the two bombs fell on Derry, two hundred tonnes of bombs were dropped on Belfast causing massive destruction and killing more than nine hundred people.

So crucial a role did Derry play in the Battle of the Atlantic that at the conclusion of the war the quayside at Lisahally was designated for the surrender of some of the German U-boats. The surrender of the first group of eight submarines was taken on 14 May 1945 by Admiral Sir Maxwell Horton, Commander-in-Chief of the Western

Surrendered U-boats in Lisahally harbour.

Approaches. The Prime Minister of Northern Ireland, Sir Basil Brooke, attended the ceremony. During the following winter, twenty-eight of these U-boats were towed out into the Atlantic and scuttled. As Derry's pivotal position in the allied war effort was being recognised, civil servants were warning that peacetime was unlikely to bring harmony to the city. At a deeper level, many of the city's structural, political and economic problems remained intact, ready to surface again as wartime prosperity melted away to be replaced by the economic depression of the 1950s and early 1960s.

The 1950s

In 1953 Eddie McAteer was elected to the Stormont Parliament for the safe Derry nationalist Foyle constituency. McAteer became leader of the Nationalist Party and, in the words of one commentator became, as did fellow Derryman John Hume two decades later, 'the image of Northern nationalism'. There were a number of incidents throughout the 1950s indicating the community rift between the city's Catholics and Protestants. There were also a few clashes between the Catholic population and the police, but nothing of a very serious or momentous nature happened. The IRA launched its 'border campaign' in the late 1950s and some incidents occurred in Derry. Several electricity installations were damaged in bomb-blasts and on one occasion a goods train was hijacked on the Great Northern line and sent driverless at full speed into the city station at Foyle Road. Once again, as on similar occasions in the past and since, local 'republicans' were interned, but the city remained comparatively quiet and, despite its problems, life went on as usual.

Housing and jobs

However, as later official reports confirmed and popular opinion at the time asserted, discrimination against Catholics, particularly in relation to jobs and housing, was widespread. The housing situation was appalling and many of the city's homeless squatted in the abandoned temporary structures erected during the war. The famous skeleton on the city's coat-of-arms was cynically said to represent a Catholic waiting for a corporation [public sector] house. Public housing was expanded when the Creggan estate was built (1947) on

the hillside overlooking the city and again, later, with the construction of the 'highflats' in Rossville Street in the Bogside in 1966. The
latter, since removed, were to feature prominently in the Battle of
the Bogside in 1969 and in the events of Bloody Sunday in 1972.

The general housing problem was exacerbated by the steady
increase in population. The 1961 census showed that the population
growth in Derry was almost twice as great as that for Northern Ireland as a whole and almost four times that for England and Wales. Of
course, most of this increase was among the poorer Catholic section
of the community. The increase in population would have been even
greater except that emigration on a record level started up again
after the war. The housing issue was greatly affected by the question
of gerrymandering. In order for the minority unionists to maintain
power in the city it was essential for them to control the mobility of
their political enemies: the nationalists or Catholics. Only house-
holders could vote in local elections, so when someone got a house it
was the same thing as getting a vote. Any movement of Catholics
between wards threatened the delicate balance which had been
achieved by the 1938 settlement. Elaborate systems of monitoring
were devised to counteract such a possibility. Equally dangerous to
the status quo was the question of expanding the boundaries of the
city and thus acquiring additional building land. Any such development would have led inevitably to the end of unionist power in the
city. One leading unionist councillor described the problem he and
his colleagues faced when he remarked, 'we are front-line unionists'.
The 1966 electoral revision showed that there were 10,000 Protestant voters in the city and twice as many Catholic voters. Nevertheless, the 1967 local elections returned a corporation made up, as
usual, of eight nationalist and twelve unionist councillors.

Despite the arrival, in 1960, of the Du Pont industrial complex
on an abandoned wartime airfield at Maydown, there was a general
atmosphere of decline and recession. Only one of the city's four original railway lines survived the 1960s. One of the city's largest employ-
ers, Monarch Electric, which made cheap record players, closed down
in 1967 throwing many hundreds onto an already long dole queue.
Other closures followed and by March 1967, at an official estimate of
just over 20 percent, the unemployment figure was double what it
had been a year earlier, three times the figure for Northern Ireland as
a whole and almost ten times the figure for Great Britain. Again, the

The Bogside and Creggan from the city walls.

Catholic population was disproportionately affected. A later investigation found that there were no Catholics at all working in the city hall (the Guildhall), and that only 30 percent of the corporation's 'white collar' workers were Catholic, although the bulk of the manual workers and the majority of the whole staff were from that section of the community.

The 'university for Derry' campaign

When the government announced that it intended to establish a second university for Northern Ireland, many assumed that it would be located in Derry, based on the existing but very small Magee College. At the time, Magee had a relationship with Trinity College in Dublin. In 1965, however, the government Lockwood Committee recommended that the new institution should be located in Coleraine. A massive cross-community campaign got under way to try to get the government to change its mind. The campaign was masterminded by a young teacher and self-help activist, John Hume. A huge motorcade went to Stormont on 18 February 1965 to press home its message. It was claimed that half the population of the city, twenty-five thousand people, made the journey.

> 'Clergy of all denominations joined with business and professional men, factory workers, dockers, school teachers and students in a motorcade which varied

from the stately limousines to furniture vans, coal lorries and bread vans ... milk vans, petrol lorries, break-
down vans and cars of every make and size.'

In the parliamentary debate which followed, the government was
criticised even from within its own ranks. A former attorney general
warned that the decision was 'political madness and the penalty will
have to be paid by the people of Northern Ireland'. The government
decision stood, however. Many would now argue that the government
scored a pyrrhic victory and that 'the university for Derry campaign'
was a form of street education in political action, the fruits of which
were to erupt in the city in the not too distant future.

1968 was 'the year of protest' against discrimination and
oppression in many parts of the world: in South Africa, in America, in
Paris, in Prague. In March of that year the Derry Housing Action
Committee (DHAC) was formed 'with the conscious intention of dis-
rupting public life in the city to draw attention to the housing problem'. The organisation caused mayhem at corporation meetings in
the Guildhall and attracted huge amounts of publicity. As the year
went on, its tactics became progressively more confrontational. In
August 1968 the first Northern Ireland Civil Rights Association
(NICRA) march, from Dungannon to Coalisland in County Tyrone,
was organised in imitation of the contemporary protests against
racial discrimination in the United States. The DHAC invited NICRA
to stage a march in Derry and fixed 5 October as the date.

5 October – the Troubles begin

The march was banned by the Home Affairs Minister, William Craig,
but the organisers decided to go ahead. Despite a campaign to
encourage participation, most people in Derry decided to ignore the
event – the Derry soccer team was playing at its home ground in the
Brandywell that Saturday. The march started in Duke Street in the
Waterside area, intending to cross the river into the old city. When
the participants reached the blockading RUC line the police
attacked. The first blows in what would become known as the Troubles had been struck. Chaos erupted with several more baton charges
throughout the rest of the evening and rioting by Catholic
youths. Similar incidents had occurred before but on this occasion,
within hours of the events, the rioting was seen all over the world as

the scenes of violence, particularly film shot by RTÉ cameraman Gay O'Brien of policemen baton-charging civilian demonstrators, were shown on television.

In the weeks that followed various meetings and demonstrations were organised and a moderate Derry Citizen's Action Committee (which included John Hume) was formed. Immediately, the local unionists began to make concessions but it was the proverbial 'too little, too late'. On 22 November the Northern Ireland government introduced a series of reforms and abolished the Londonderry corporation. The Prime Minister of Northern Ireland, Captain Terence O'Neill, made a famous broadcast (in his no doubt sincere but, unfortunately, whining voice) pleading with the people of Northern Ireland to step back from the brink of disaster.

Burntollett

A truce was called but on New Year's Day 1969 a group of left-wing student activists began a march from Belfast to Derry to draw attention to the repressive nature of the state. The march was harassed along the route before being viciously attacked at Burntollet Bridge, a few miles outside Derry. There were allegations that the police had colluded with those who opposed the march and in the city the inevitable rioting began. At 2.00am on the following morning a group of policemen invaded the Bogside and

Burntollet, January 1969.

caused havoc. The government Cameron Commission later found that:

> 'a number of policemen were guilty of misconduct which involved assault and battery, malicious damage to property ... and the use of provocative sectarian and political slogans.'

It was on the following day that the famous slogan, 'You are now entering Free Derry', was painted on a gable wall in the Bogside. The slogan, which was an imitation of the more famous original in Berlin, was intended to indicate that the writ of the RUC did not apply in the Catholic ghetto areas of Derry. It would eventually become a symbol of the so-called 'no-go' area of the Bogside. The wall, with its slogan, still survives and is now preserved as a historic monument.

At the February elections for the Northern Ireland Parliament, John Hume, standing as an independent, took the seat for the Foyle constituency from Eddie McAteer. The torch had passed to a new generation.

The corporation had been replaced by an appointed Londonderry Development Commission which began to tackle the city's huge backlog of problems. Riots flared again on 19 April when the government banned another civil rights march. Police invaded the home of a local man in the Bogside, Samuel Devenney, and beat him up. He died three months later of a heart condition which, it was alleged, was brought on by the treatment he had received from the RUC. The investigating police found a 'conspiracy of silence' among members of their own organisation concerning the incident and no charges were ever brought. Riots continued and tension mounted in the lead up to that year's annual march by the Apprentice Boys, scheduled for Tuesday, 12 August. In the Bogside, stashes of petrol bombs and other home-made weapons were prepared and contact was made with the Irish government requesting southern intervention in the event of another expected police attack.

The 'Battle of the Bogside'

On the day of the march the inevitable rioting began. Catholic youths began throwing petrol bombs and the RUC responded with CS gas. The 'Battle of the Bogside' would last for three days. On the evening of the second day, Taoiseach Jack Lynch made a broadcast stating that the Dublin government 'could not stand by'. Field hospitals were opened by the southern authorities in nearby County Donegal and Irish diplomats abroad attempted to exert some indirect pressure on the British government.

As the situation deteriorated, nationalist leaders, including

John Hume and Bernadette Devlin, called for the intervention of the British Army. After three days, with the police in Derry in a state of exhaustion, the Northern Ireland government also requested military assistance. At 5.00pm on Thursday, 14 August 1969, a company of the Prince of Wales' Own Regiment took over security control from the RUC in the centre of Derry. The so-called 'no-go' areas [for the police] were established immediately. Almost thirty years later British troops are still involved in the north 'in support of the civil authority', albeit in increasingly reduced numbers and in less prominent roles. Some of the Bogside residents who watched the troops arriving on that August day were initially unsure whether they were British or Irish soldiers. In the weeks which followed

The Battle of the Bogside, 1969.

there was the famous 'honeymoon period' in which soldiers were welcomed and plied with cups of tea and buns. The British Home Secretary, James Callaghan, came to Derry and, from the upstairs window of a Bogside house, told the hordes of highly emotional people, in a somewhat patronising tone,

> 'You have engaged my sympathies and my energies. I will try and ensure that there is justice and equality, absence of fear and discrimination ...'

The 'Provisionals': internment

While things had been happening in Derry – the 'cockpit' of the Troubles – the conflict had also spread to Belfast and other parts of Northern Ireland. By now the situation had its own dynamic; relations between the Catholic community and the army deteriorated. The republican movement split and the Provisional IRA was established. People were killed on both sides and the newly-founded SDLP (Social, Democratic and Labour Party, an umbrella party originally formed from a range of nationalist and independent political views), withdrew from the Stormont Parliament.

British soldiers in the city.

On 9 August 1971 the government introduced internment without trial which applied exclusively to Catholic 'suspects' despite the well-known existence of Protestant paramilitaries. The policy turned out to be a political and security disaster. The British government was later found guilty by the European Court of Human Rights of the 'inhuman and degrading treatment' of its prisoners. The 'intelligence' used to identify those to be arrested was totally inaccurate. The result was widespread alienation of the nationalist population and the intensification of republican violence, particularly against so-called 'economic targets', as retail and business premises came to be known. Well-known landmarks disappeared under piles of rubble. 'Shop now, while shops last' was not just a piece of traditional, cynical Derry wit.

Bloody Sunday, Bloody Friday and Operation Motorman

On Sunday, 30 January 1972 – Bloody Sunday – the 1st Battalion of the Parachute Regiment fired on civilians taking part in a NICRA anti-internment rally. Thirteen men were killed and another fourteen seriously wounded, one of whom died later. The consequences of Bloody Sunday have still not been played out and (in early 1999), official enquiries into the events of that day are still ongoing. Aside from the personal tragedies, the abolition of the Stormont Parliament was probably the most dramatic outcome of those events.

The situation continued to deteriorate. The Official IRA bombed the British Army base at Aldershot in Hampshire in revenge for Bloody Sunday, and in May killed a local Derry Catholic, Ranger Best, who was home on leave from the British Army. The killing shocked the city and thousands protested against the violence. Attempts were made to persuade the British government to talk with the paramilitaries. Among those involved in these initial moves towards negotiations were John Hume and Martin McGuinness. McGuinness is now Sinn Féin's chief negotiator in the current peace process. The Provisional IRA declared a ceasefire from midnight on 26 June 1972 and plans were made for a secret meeting in London with representatives of the British government. The meeting was held on 7 July and the IRA delegation included Gerry Adams and Martin McGuinness. The leading British representative was the Secretary of State for Northern Ireland, William Whitelaw. The meeting ended without agreement and the ceasefire broke down two days later as a result of an incident in Lenadoon in Belfast. The violence intensified and on 21 July – Bloody Friday – twenty Provisional IRA bombs exploded in Belfast city centre in the space of an hour. Nine people were killed and at least 130 were seriously injured.

Martin McGuinness helping to clear a border obstacle near Derry.

At 4.30am on 31 July 1972, the British Army commenced Operation Motorman against the 'no-go' areas of Belfast and Derry. Twelve thousand troops were involved in what has been claimed was the largest British military operation since the Suez crisis of 1956. The ad hoc barricades erected to keep the security forces out of the ghetto areas were removed. But the army failed to capture any members of the IRA – one of the principal aims of the manoeuvre – and two civilians were killed. In retaliation, republican car bombs, set off in the little village of Claudy, a few miles east of Derry, killed nine civilians.

The past thirty years

It would be impossible to give here a detailed account of all the incidents of the Troubles during the 1970s and 1980s. Apart from anything else, there is still too much controversy and pain surrounding them to be able to arrive at an objective narrative. About 7 percent of all violent deaths in the Northern Ireland Troubles occurred in Derry. In addition, thousands were injured or otherwise affected and damage to property was substantial.

However, these years were not without some positive out-comes. In 1973 the City Council was restored and, operating by and large on a local power-sharing basis, it has been responsible for many improvements in the city. Housing has been greatly improved and, freed from the constraints of the gerrymander, the city has (meta-phorically) exploded in all directions. There have been many achieve-ments in education, in sport and cultural life and, since the mid-1980s, huge attempts have been made to rebuild and restore the ruined city.

John Hume MEP and MP, leader of the SDLP.

By 1980 it was claimed that as much as 30 per-cent of the downtown area of the city had been destroyed as a direct result of the violence. Much of the remaining 70 percent in the centre of the city had deteriorated from the associated depression and neglect. But the restoration of the historic city centre has been led by sensible public policies and by the more imaginative schemes of one of the city's best-known 'community entrepreneurs', Paddy 'Bog-side' Doherty. Nowadays, if for any reason you wanted to find one, it would be hard to come across a bomb-site in Derry.

For all intents and purposes, the Troubles were over in Derry (with the exception of a few incidents), by about 1984. One of the saddest consequences of the Troubles in the city has been the drift of the city's Protestant population to the east bank of the river, away from the historic areas with which they were previ-ously associated. The population on the 'west bank of the Foyle' now almost exactly mirrors the demographic structure of the Republic of Ireland in terms of age and religious denomination.

Despite everything that history, and particularly modern his-tory, has thrown at it, Derry still retains much of its original charm and traditional atmosphere. It is now a vibrant, friendly and beautiful city, full of interesting buildings and energetic people. The city is famous for its self-help and community-based organisations and proj-ects, not to mention its thriving arts and cultural life. With peace now virtually assured, the city still awaits its economic renaissance, but it seems certain that it will have a much brighter, better future to go along with its fascinating past.

Above and below: The city walls.
Built between 1613 and 1618, they are the only surviving complete city walls in Ireland.

Craigavon Bridge, opened in 1933 to replace its predecessor, the Carlisle Bridge. The lower deck on both bridges was built to carry railway locomotives.

The river Foyle. A wide, fast-flowing river, although only about twenty miles long, the Foyle is formed by the union of the rivers Finn and Mourne upstream.

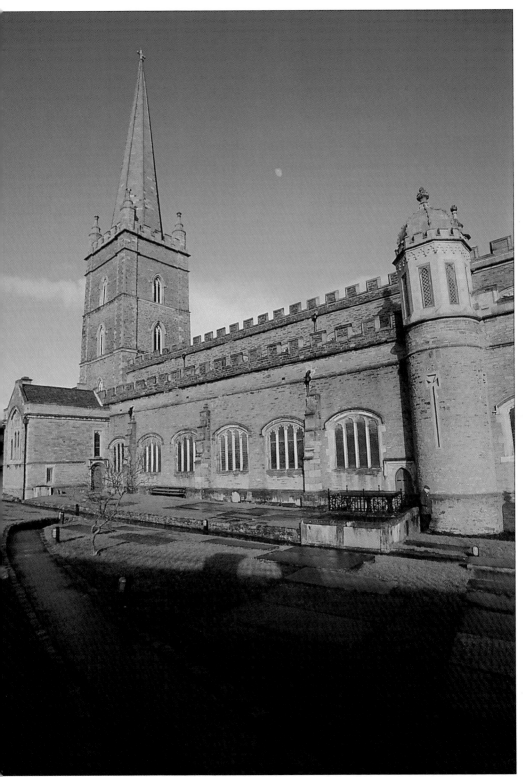

St Columb's Cathedral. Built as the city's Protestant cathedral between 1628 and 1633.
It is one of the most important seventeenth-century buildings in Ireland.

Above: The 'Long Tower' Church. One of the best-loved buildings in the city, it was rebuilt in its present guise in 1909. It stands on the site of a previous building, originally erected in 1784. The site has been used for ecclesiastical purposes since the twelfth century, at least.

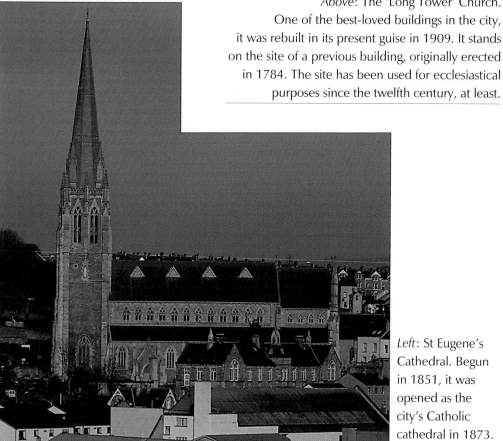

Left: St Eugene's Cathedral. Begun in 1851, it was opened as the city's Catholic cathedral in 1873.

St Brecan's Church. The remains of the church stand in the centre of St Columb's Park.
The ruins would appear to date to the late sixteenth century.

The Bogside from the city walls with St Eugene's Cathedral, centre.
The stump of the former Walker Pillar is visible on the right.

The workhouse.
Opened originally in 1840, the building was reopened as a library and museum in 1998.

The Guildhall or city hall. Originally built in 1890, rebuilt after a fire in 1908 and extensively refurbished after bomb damage in 1972. The clock-tower is the biggest of its kind in Ireland.

Tillie and Henderson's shirt-factory.
Built in 1856 to a design by the local architect and
controversial public figure, John Guy Ferguson.

Opposite: View of the city of Derry
from the high ground on the east
bank of the river Foyle.

Austin's Department Store. Built in 1906, it is one of Derry's most prominent buildings.

Waterloo Street. A traditional Derry street, full of small shops and lively pubs.

Magee College. Now part of the University of Ulster, it was originally founded as a Presbyterian theological and liberal arts college in 1865.

Lumen Christi College, formerly St Columb's College, one of the city's best-known
educational institutions. It boasts two Nobel prizewinners among its alumni.

Bishop St, looking north towards the Diamond and the Guildhall.
The courthouse, built in 1817, is on the right.

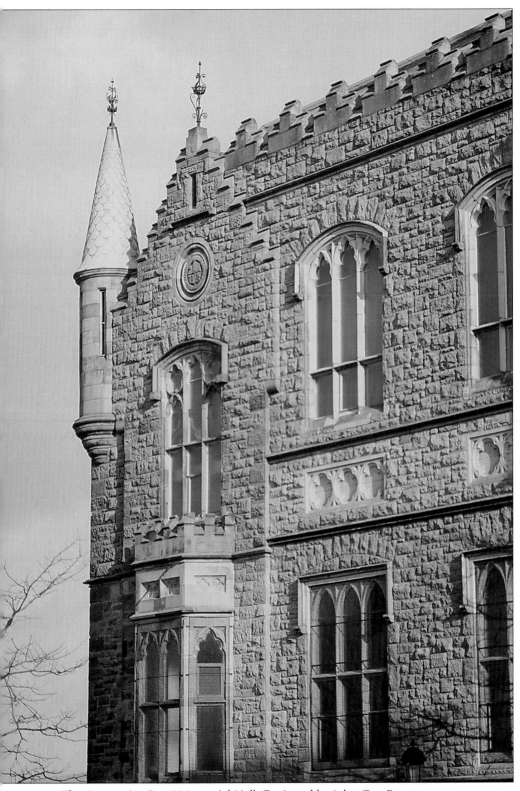
The Apprentice Boys' Memorial Hall. Designed by John Guy Ferguson, the 'Mem' was originally built in 1873. It was extended considerably in 1937.

Left and below: The Tower Museum. Opened in 1992, it is the only institution to have been both British and Irish Museum of the Year.

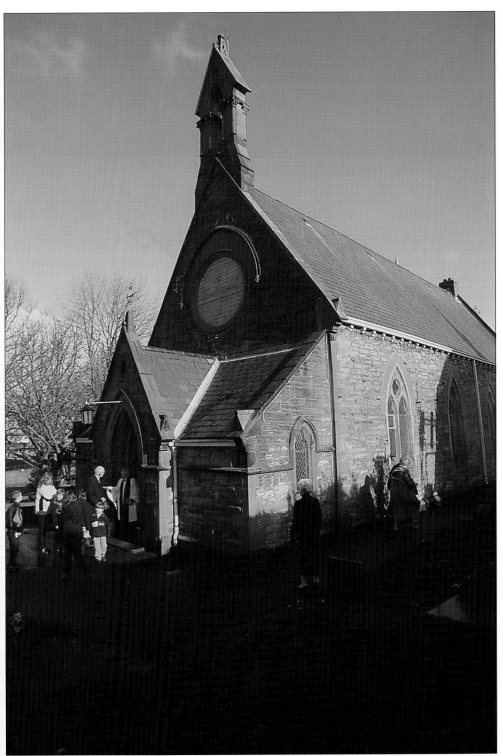

St Augustine's Church takes its name from the medieval Augustinian Abbey which stood on this site. The present building was erected in 1872, but the site has probably been in use for ecclesiastical purposes for well over a thousand years.

A wall mural in the Bogside depicting Bernadette Devlin, the well-known civil rights leader.

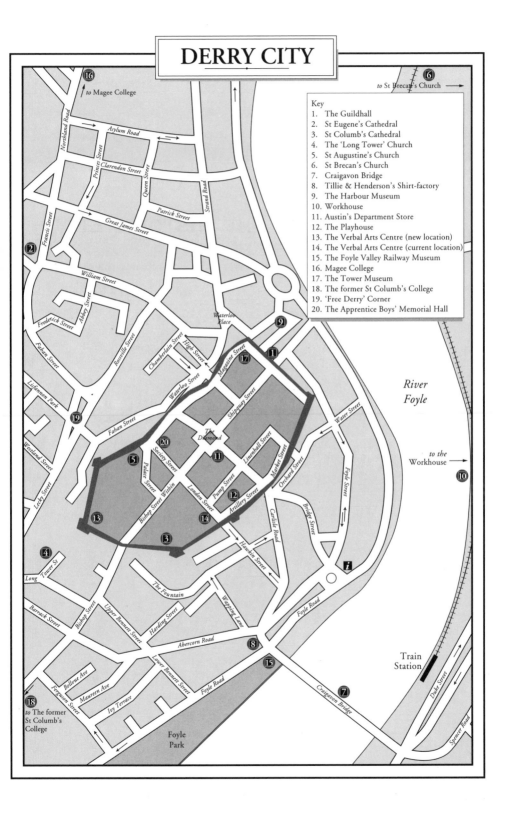

DERRY CITY

Key
1. The Guildhall
2. St Eugene's Cathedral
3. St Columb's Cathedral
4. The 'Long Tower' Church
5. St Augustine's Church
6. St Brecan's Church
7. Craigavon Bridge
8. Tillie & Henderson's Shirt-factory
9. The Harbour Museum
10. Workhouse
11. Austin's Department Store
12. The Playhouse
13. The Verbal Arts Centre (new location)
14. The Verbal Arts Centre (current location)
15. The Foyle Valley Railway Museum
16. Magee College
17. The Tower Museum
18. The former St Columb's College
19. 'Free Derry' Corner
20. The Apprentice Boys' Memorial Hall

GUIDE TO THE HISTORIC CITY

THE CITY WALLS

Londonderry is the last city in Ireland to be encircled by walls. It is the only city or town in Ireland where the original walls survive intact and, arguably, it must be one of the few places in the world where the ancient walls still performed some of their original defensive purposes until relatively recently.

For thousands of years, since the very beginning of urbanism, the walled city had stood as a symbol of civilisation – the city delimited and defined against those wilder, perhaps 'barbaric', forces outside. With developments in artillery at the close of the Middle Ages and the beginning of the Renaissance, the idea of defending a city with stout walls became increasingly irrelevant. However, the conditions under which the colonising project known as the Plantations was organised in Ulster at the beginning of the seventeenth century, and the relative underdevelopment in these matters of the native Gaelic population, meant that measures which were almost redundant elsewhere were pressed into service here.

The city walls.

Early Irish monasteries were usually enclosed by an encircling wall or bank, although the extent to which this was thought of either in defensive or ritual terms is open to question. We know that in Derry in 1162 the then abbot, Flaithbertach O'Brolcháin, built a wall to separate the ecclesiastical buildings from the secular areas of the settlement. Whatever the extent of that wall, O'Brolcháin decided to bolster its actual defensiveness with the added weight of a malediction on anyone who would violate it!

When King James I granted a charter to the 'city of Derrie' in 1604 he described it as:

> By reason of the natural seat and situation thereof, a place very convenient and fit to be made both a town of war and a town of merchandize, and so might many ways prove serviceable for the Crown and profitable for the subject, if the same were not only walled, entrenched and inhabited, but also incorporated and endowed with convenient liberties, privileges and immunities ...

That 'city' was destroyed by Sir Cahir O'Doherty's attack in 1608 but was replaced by the more elaborate, and better defended, walled colonial city of Londonderry, begun in 1611. The walls themselves were built between 1613 and 1618, at a total cost of £10,357, under the supervision of Peter Benson, a master bricklayer and tiler from London. They were designed by Sir Edward Doddington whose house, at the former Augustinian priory in Dungiven, County Derry, was excavated in the mid-1980s. The detailed survey work associated with the construction of the walls was carried out by Thomas Raven, official surveyor of the City of London, many of whose maps and plans for the Londonderry plantation still survive.

The walls originally consisted of a twelve-foot thick earthen/rubble rampart, faced externally by a six-foot deep stone 'skin'. For much of their length there was a fosse or dry ditch along the outside of the walls, the original excavation of which produced the material for the inner earthen core. This ditch was not continued along the north-western section of the walls which overlooks part of the Bogside area. Traditionally, the core of the walls along this section is said to have been derived from the rubble of medieval and other buildings destroyed in the 1608 attack. Lengthy and careful examination of the walls along this section, however, has failed to turn up any traces of obvious medieval stone. An alternative explanation for the lack of a fosse along this section would be that the hillside drops away very steeply here, immediately outside the walls. A report about this section, made in 1616, seems to have been prophetic:

And whereas it was formerly agreed that on the hill
towards the bog [the Bogside] the height of the wall
should be but 16 foot high which upon view was
found to be very low and not defensive we have therefore directed that the wall in that place and in other
places where need shall be 19 foot high from the face
of the earth and no ditch be made there but the hill
scarped.

On several occasions over the past thirty years the security
forces have found it necessary to 'raise the height' of the wall here
with additional defences.

Ferryquay Gate.

The walls' inner 'skin' of stone and many of the steps up onto
them are not original. Neither are any of the main gates. Originally
there were only four defended gates through the walls, each facing
one of the four main streets which divide the inner city into quarters.
A small, arched postern gate through the wall along the Upper Foun-
tain section seems to be the oldest exit and may date to the early part
of the seventeenth century. The present gates (of which there are six,
with an additional, non-structural crossing point), were redesigned
at various periods in the eighteenth and nineteenth centuries to
facilitate movement in and out of the historic city and, in a few cases,
to act as commemorative monuments.

The layout of the walls has often been criticised from a military
point of view. The highest point of the hill on which they are built

actually lies outside the walls and many of the nearby surrounding hills are higher again, exposing the fortified city to the possibility of cannon fire from both sides of the river. This has often given rise to the suggestion that the overall design of the city and its walls may actually have been laid down on paper in London by people who had never seen the actual location and who, therefore, would have had little appreciation of the local topography. Whatever their limitations, the walls of Derry became vitally important both to citizens and to garrisons when the city was besieged twice during the seventeenth century – first by royalist Presbyterian forces in 1649 who opposed the parliamentarians inside the city, and secondly during the siege of 1689 when Jacobite forces loyal to James II attempted to capture the city and its Williamite defenders.

There were several other occasions when it was thought that the walls would be required to defend the city, such as from the threat of a feared French invasion in 1798. The walls have even provided a useful vantage point and defensive position for the security forces over the course of the Troubles of the past thirty years.

On a number of occasions in the nineteenth century, local businessmen argued for the demolition of the city walls in order to open the town up and thereby improve commerce. But the walls have survived all attempts to remove them and now, like the legendary painting work on the Forth Bridge in Scotland, there is a permanent team of workmen who repair and conserve the walls continuously, starting on one section as soon as they have finished another. In our times, the walls have served as a spectacular promenade, a line of defence, a stage for theatrical presentations, a course for joggers, a gallery for artworks and, at times, as a contested route for marchers and protesters. Most of all they serve as an extraordinary and unique historical monument to a fascinating part of our heritage.

THE GUILDHALL

From the seventeenth until the late nineteenth century a succession of Derry's town halls had been located in the Diamond, the central square of the walled city. In 1887 work commenced on a new building on land outside the walls which originally had been part of the tidal slobs of the river. Since the seventeenth century the river bank had gradually been pushed outwards, facilitating the expanding docks and warehouse buildings. The new town hall, the Guildhall (it was named after its counterpart in the City of London and because of the Londonderry association), was opened in 1890. However, in a disastrous fire on Easter Sunday, 19 April 1908 the building was destroyed. Contemporary commentators argued that the corporation's neglect of the fire service, and of adequate water supplies, contributed to the damage to their own headquarters. Reconstruction began immediately and by 1913 the building was fully operative again.

The Guildhall was massively damaged again in 1972 when, twice in the same week, IRA bombs were detonated in the building. Ironically, in 1985 Gerry Doherty was elected as a member of the City Council. He had previously served a term of imprisonment, having been convicted of taking part in the bombing of the Guildhall, where he was now sitting as a Sinn Féin councillor.

A stone carving of St Colmcille in the Guildhall.

The Guildhall is the ceremonial seat of the government of the city (since 1996 the actual administration has been carried on from the impressive new Civic Offices on the bank of the river Foyle about half a mile downstream). The building contains the Council

Chamber, party offices and a major and minor assembly hall at first floor level, as well as some other offices and reception rooms. The Guildhall is noted for its fittings and finishes, especially its marvellous collection of stained glass and its wonderful concert organ. The Big Ben style clock-tower (the largest of its kind in Ireland), is a distinctive landmark which can be seen from many parts of the city, such that it has become something of a local symbol.

The building is a true town hall with all sorts of events taking place there from civic receptions for VIPs, such as President Bill Clinton, to concerts, community dances, exhibitions and graduation ceremonies for both Magee University College and the North West College of Technology. In the 1980s the Guildhall was the venue for a series of world premières by the distinguished Field Day Theatre Company which included Brian Friel's famous play, *Translations*. The Mayor's parlour, beside the Council Chamber, is itself the locale for the action of another of Friel's plays, *Freedom of the City*.

THE COAT-OF-ARMS

The city's coat-of-arms was granted by Dan Molineux, Ulster King of Armes, on 1 June 1613. It is made up of two distinct sections. The top half ('a chiefe of London'), is derived from the insignia of the City of London. The lower half is the older arms of Derry. The two together thus make up the coat-of-arms of the City of Londonderry.

Greencastle, County Donegal, built by the de Burgos.

It is not known how old the Derry section is (it may only date to the time of Sir Henry Docwra, c.1603) but clearly it is older than the plantation period. The exact meaning of the skeletal figure of 'Death sitting on a mossie stone' is not known but it is often humorously interpreted as a citizen waiting to be attended by a slow or discriminatory municipal bureaucracy. Traditionally it is said to represent the real historical figure of Walter de Burgo who died in 1332 at the fortification at Greencastle in County Donegal (the former castle of Northburgh). This castle had been built in 1305 by Richard de Burgo, Earl of Ulster. Richard was granted land at Derry, where he had had a previous involvement, by King Edward II in 1311. Walter de Burgo died of starvation there when, in the course of a family feud, he was immured in the walls of the castle. The Latin motto on the coat-of-arms translates as 'Life, Truth, Victory'.

ST EUGENE'S CATHEDRAL

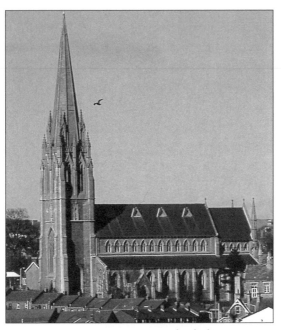

St Eugene's Cathedral.

Like most of the Catholic cathedrals in Ireland, St Eugene's is a nineteenth-century Gothic revival building. Construction work on the cathedral, at its elevated site overlooking the Bogside district, was begun in 1851 by the newly-appointed bishop, Dr Francis Kelly. Dr Kelly is also remembered for introducing a number of welfare and educational institutions to the city to help cope with the growing Catholic population, many of whom were extremely poor. These organisations included the Sisters of Mercy, the Irish Christian Brothers and the Society of St Vincent de Paul.

The cathedral was finally opened in 1873 but it was another thirty years before it acquired its magnificent 256-foot tall spire. The building has been extensively refurbished in the past few years.

The cathedral derived its name from the ancient monastery of Ardstraw which had been founded by St Eoghan (latinised: Eugenius), even though we might have expected that it would have been dedicated to St Colmcille or Columba, the patron saint of Derry.

The first seat of the bishopric, which would eventually evolve into the diocese of Derry, was at Ardstraw in County Tyrone. It was subsequently moved to Maghera in County Derry, before moving again in the thirteenth century into the city of Derry. The reasons for all these moves had as much to do with the secular politics of the time as with ecclesiastical matters.

St Eugene's is the Catholic cathedral of the diocese of Derry. The diocese of Derry is a totally different entity to the county of Derry. The diocese includes the Inishowen peninsula and other parts of County Donegal as well as some areas in County Tyrone. The explanation for this is that all the dioceses in Ireland came into existence long before the counties were delimited. The dioceses are based on medieval Gaelic political units rather than the requirements of English colonial administration, which gave us the shape of our counties. The diocese of Derry most likely represents the territory claimed by the Ua Lochlainn kings (who lived in Derry itself) in the twelfth century.

ST COLUMB'S CATHEDRAL

St Columb's is the Church of Ireland (Anglican) cathedral of the diocese of Derry. It was built between 1628 and 1633. It seems to have been the first specially-built cathedral erected anywhere in these islands following the Protestant Reformation as, in most cases, the existing medieval cathedral buildings were inherited by the established, reformed church. The site chosen for St Columb's was the highest point inside the walled city, almost the highest point on the hill of Derry. The cathedral, with its elegant tower and spire, can still be seen for miles around.

St Columb's Cathedral
viewed from the Waterside.

The cathedral was built at the expense of the London companies which had sponsored the Londonderry plantation and the building of the walled city. For this reason, it might be worth pointing out that from the outset the cathedral has been dedicated to the old Irish saint, Colmcille – we might have expected its London patrons to have favoured a saint more familiar to themselves such as St Paul or St George. It is not certain, but seems likely, that the cathedral is built on or close to the site of a medieval church which is shown on a number of maps made at the beginning of the seventeenth century. In the entrance vestibule there is a small stone plaque which carries the inscription: *In Templo/Verus Deus/Est Vereque/Colendus* – 'the true God is in the church and truly he is to be worshipped'. This stone is said to have been taken from the destroyed medieval cathedral church of Derry, the Tempull Mór, erected in the twelfth century and destroyed in 1567. However, the style of the lettering on the stone does not suggest that it came from a Gaelic source.

This alleged medieval stone is framed inside a seventeenth-century inscribed stone which carries a famous dedication verse:

If stones could speake
Then Londons prayse
Should sound who
Built this church and
Cittie from the grounde.

The cathedral was built by one William Parrott under the general supervision of Sir John Vaughan. It cost £3,800 to complete and, five years after it was finished, King Charles I presented a set of seven bells which cost another £500. Although it has been much altered in subsequent years, the building is nevertheless one of the most important surviving seventeenth-century structures in Ireland. It is basically a typical London church dating to a period from which few of the genuine articles survive because of the great fire of London in 1666. Among the more recent additions are the spire and the Chapter House, which now houses a small museum filled with fascinating memorabilia.

The building played an extremely important role in the events surrounding the Siege of Derry in 1689. Many items deriving from that period are displayed in the cathedral including a hollow cannonball in which Jacobite surrender terms were fired into the city. Among the distinguished individuals associated with the cathedral is George Berkeley, the philosopher, who was (for the most part absentee) Dean here from 1724 to 1732. The husband of Mrs Alexander, the writer of such famous hymns as *Once in Royal David's City* and *There is a Green Hill Far Away,* was bishop here in the late nineteenth century.

THE 'LONG TOWER' CHURCH

The walled city had been founded in the seventeenth century as a distinctly Protestant colony, therefore, very few Catholics lived inside the walls. During times of crisis those Catholics who did, principally servants of various kinds, were expelled from the city. However, as the eighteenth century progressed the number of Catholics living immediately outside the walls began to increase, especially in the area later to become known as the Bogside. The Bogside began its history as a kind of Soweto, a poor and unenfranchised Catholic ghetto. By the 1780s, when the Penal Laws were relaxed, the residents of this ghetto were ministered to by their parish priest, Fr John Lynch, who, along with his bishop, Dr Philip McDevitt, had taken the oath of allegiance to the Crown in 1782. Fr Lynch is purported to have said his masses under a well-known hawthorn tree at a site in the area which had been used for ecclesiastical purposes since at least the twelfth century.

The 'Long Tower' Church.

Around this time a spirit of enlightenment and tolerance had developed in the city, fostered by the Protestant bishop, the eccentric and enigmatic Frederick Augustus Hervey – the 'earl bishop' (as well as being Bishop of Derry he was also Earl of Bristol). Supported by Hervey and by the all-Protestant corporation of the city, Fr Lynch began building a church beside the beloved hawthorn tree in 1784. Bishop Hervey is said to have donated £200 (a large sum in those days) to the building fund, as well as four Corinthian columns which he had brought especially from Naples. These columns still frame the high altar of the church. The corporation gave £50 to the project.

The 'Long Tower' church, as it came to be known, derived its name from the medieval round tower which had stood nearby and which had survived until the middle of the seventeenth century. It was the first Catholic church to be erected in Derry following the plantation period. It was situated on or near the location of the great medieval cathedral of Derry, the Tempull Mór (literally 'great church' or 'big church'), which had been erected in 1164 and had become the cathedral of the diocese of Derry about one hundred years later.

Despite the building of St Eugene's cathedral in the 1850s and other churches in the city, the 'Long Tower' remained at the heart of Derry Catholicism, as it does to the present day. Part of the reason for this was that tradition had it that this was the site of the original Columban monastery of Derry. One of the priests who was administrator there at the turn of this century, Fr William Doherty, helped to foster that tradition. Fr Doherty had the church reconstructed and refurbished between 1907 and 1909, using magnificent stained glass and other exquisite decorative detail to retell the legendary story of St Colmcille's foundation of the monastery of Derry on that very spot. However, Fr Doherty was almost certainly mistaken, both about the identity of the founder of the monastery and about the location. It is widely accepted that the first monastic church of Derry was located where St Augustine's Church of Ireland chapel-of-ease now stands.

It is easy, with hindsight, to be critical of Fr Doherty. He had a tremendous devotion to the saint which may have led him to make unwarranted conclusions. However, equally one would have to say that, in the more sectarian atmosphere of those times, Derry Catholics would have found it hard to accept that the site of the 'original' foundation of the monastery, by the man they believed to be their patron saint, was by then occupied by a Protestant church. Fr Doherty's legacy lives on in the elaborate neo-Renaissance style of the 'Long Tower' church, which is still one of the best-loved structures in Derry.

Just below the church, down a set of steps, a footpath leads across to St Columb's Well. Nowadays, a nineteenth-century cast-iron pump marks the spot. In medieval times there were three 'holy wells' here, dedicated respectively to St Adomnán, St Martin and St Colmcille. Adomnán, who was a relative of Colmcille, became ninth abbot of Iona in AD 679 and also wrote a Life of his illustrious ancestor. St Martin, who was bishop of Tours in France in the fourth century and who had been among the first to introduce monasticism into western Christianity, was a much respected figure in the Irish church in early and medieval times.

Also to be seen near the holy well is the modern sculptured pillar by the Slovenian artist, Marko Pogacnic. Other examples of Pogacnic's work, which he believes has a 'healing' influence on the landscape similar to the effect of acupuncture on the human body, can be seen at several locations in Derry and in its immediate hinterland.

ST AUGUSTINE'S CHURCH

This beautiful little chapel-of-ease, situated just off the city walls, was constructed in the late nineteenth century. It is located on a site which has been in continuous use for ecclesiastical purposes since medieval times at least, and almost certainly for well over a thousand years. Despite some traditions to the contrary, it may well be that this is the site of the original monastery founded in Derry in the sixth century.

In the thirteenth century, the old Columban monastery in Derry, and its counterparts in other parts of Ireland, adopted the Rule of St Augustine, embracing the continental style of Augustinian monasticism. The older, Irish-style monastery in Derry was known as the Dub Regles, or 'Black Church', and throughout the Middle Ages was believed to have been founded by St Colmcille himself. Whatever the facts of its origin or age, it must have been a fairly ancient foundation because when it burned down in 1166 (apparently accidentally), the chronicler added that this was 'something which had not been heard of since ancient times'.

Subsequent references to the Dub Regles in the later Middle Ages equate this building with the Augustinian church. There is a fairly comprehensive account of a visit to the monastery in 1397 by the Englishman John Colton, the then Archbishop of Armagh. When

St Augustine's Church and the rector,
Reverend Rosemary Logue.

he stayed at the Augustinian monastery in Derry he was obliged to draw up a set of regulations to improve the moral behaviour of the monks there. Incidentally, in 1382, before Colton became Archbishop, he had served as Justiciar or head of the king's government in Ireland; he was, therefore, the only person in Irish history to have attained the most senior ecclesiastical as well as the most senior secular position in the country.

The Augustinian monastery survived until the beginning of the seventeenth century when it is shown, together with its ancillary buildings, on a number of English maps of Derry, as well as being referred to in the contemporary English and Gaelic documentation. When Sir Cahir O'Doherty attacked the little English colonial 'city of Derrie' in 1608, he destroyed almost every building in the settlement, but he spared the Dub Regles. An excusably hostile witness wrote that the church 'whose timber work, either in respect of the height or in their devotion to their solemn Colmcille, the patron of that place, and whose name they use as their word of privity and distinction in all their wicked and treacherous attempts, was not fired'.

It appears that the medieval church was refurbished and served as the first church of the settlers who came over subsequently from Britain to live in the plantation city of Londonderry. It was the only church in the city until St Columb's Cathedral was completed in 1633. As far as we can determine, the medieval church continued to stand until the middle of the eighteenth century, when it was replaced. The present church succeeded the latter building in 1872. The church and its graveyard are situated in a picturesque location and contain a number of interesting memorial stones.

FOYLE ARTS CENTRE

The Foyle Arts Centre is located in the former Foyle College building on a hillside overlooking the river Foyle, just north of the historic area of the city. It is situated opposite the new Civic Offices which house the principal administrative centre of the city. Foyle College itself, which has now moved to another site on the outskirts of the city, was a Protestant boys' grammar school but has now merged with the former (girls') Londonderry High School to become a co-educational (and, one might add, mixed religion) institution. The building was erected in 1814 and continued as a school until the 1960s, after which it became derelict. The restoration of the building and the development of the organisation which undertook that task, the North West Centre for Learning and Development, under the leadership of the redoubtable Paddy 'Bogside' Doherty, was one of the most important 'good news' stories to have come out of the city at the height of the Troubles. This body was set up as a combination of a radical 'second chance' education institution and a job skills opportunity facility. It has gone on to undertake many other reconstruction and construction projects, particularly within the city's walled area, playing an enormously important role in the regeneration of the city.

Foyle College was the linear descendant of the seventeenth-century Free School which had been located in Society Street, inside the walled city. That school had been set up thanks to a donation, in 1616, by Matthias Springham, who was an 'assistant' or senior officer in The Irish Society – the body which was charged with the establishment of the Londonderry colony. Among the exceptional pupils of that school was the Restoration dramatist, George Farquhar. Foyle College itself had many distinguished pupils, among them the songwriter Percy French, the revolutionary John Mitchell, the great classicist and historian James Bury, and the Lawrence brothers who had important careers as colonial administrators.

The Wrestlers, by F.E. McWilliams, outside The Foyle Arts Centre.

Following its restoration, the building began to be used as a general arts centre, operated by the City Council. All sorts of activities go on there, both amateur and professional. The Derry offices of the famous Field Day Theatre and Publishing Company are located here. The building contains several gallery/studio spaces, recording studios and audio-visual facilities, as well as two small theatre spaces.

ST BRECAN'S CHURCH

The largest park in the city, St Columb's Park, is located on the east bank of the river Foyle in the Waterside area. The trees of the park are visible across the river from the Shipquay Place area and the Guildhall. In the centre of the park lie the very ruined remains of St Brecan's Church. Not much is known about St Brecan and, both in ancient and modern times, the church is sometimes said to be named after the better-known St Colmcille. The precise date of the surviving structure has not been determined but it appears to pre-date the end of the sixteenth century at least. Whatever the date of the building, it is located at the site of the ancient church referred to from the twelfth century onwards as Cluain Í, which lends its name in the anglicised form of Clooney to the surrounding area.

There is an extraordinary description of a visit, on Sunday, 14 October 1397, to the 'parish church of St Brecan' by the Archbishop of Armagh, John Colton. One Sunday morning the Archbishop was rowed across to the east bank of the river, as requested by 'Dr William Mac Cathmhaoil, Dean of the Cathedral church of Derry', to reconsecrate St Brecan's which had been 'polluted' by the shedding of blood there. Thousands of people turned up and a temporary altar had to be set up outside the tiny church for the celebration of mass. During the mass the Archbishop installed Hugh Mac Gillibride as abbot of the Dub Regles or 'Black Church'. Among the other unusual matters dealt with at the mass was a request from the bishop of the neighbouring diocese of Raphoe for Dr Colton to absolve from excommunication the members of the 'Chapter of Derry' on whom he had imposed that penalty the day before. The differences between the Archbishop and the Chapter related mainly to matters of property in the diocese. Colton relented and instructed the Bishop of Raphoe to attend to the matter himself and to remove the interdict according to the rites of the church and 'under pain and condition nevertheless of falling a second time under the same sentence, if they did not afterwards obey the mandates and ordinances of the Lord Archbishop'.

In 1466 another Englishman (or possibly a member of the so-called 'Old English in Ireland'), Nicholas Weston, became Bishop of Derry. Weston remained in his post until his death in 1484 and seems to have fitted into the diocese very well, but there is a very curious reference to him in the *Life of Colmcille* written in 1532 by Manus O'Donnell. O'Donnell relates a (fictional) story, partly in verse, of how, in the sixth century, Colmcille had predicted that a 'foreign' bishop would come and destroy the church at Clooney:

> My fear is that foreign strangers,
> Here to Clooney, yet will come,
> And bear my church away with them,
> To Bun Sentuinne, cold and numb.

St Brecan's Church.

The name Bun Sentuinne is now lost but it was probably a place very close to Clooney on the bank of the river Foyle. It appears that Weston started to build a 'palace' for himself there, allegedly using some of the stones of the church which, presumably, was ruined at the time. Manus O'Donnell records that, through a miracle of (the allegedly disgusted) Colmcille, the palace was never finished. It is likely that the church was reconstructed later in the sixteenth century and that the remains we see today belong to that later structure. Near to the ruined church and also inside the park is St Columb's House, a peace and reconciliation conference centre.

THE BRIDGES

Despite the fact that a relatively major settlement had existed at Derry since at least the end of the sixth century, the first bridge to be built across the river Foyle was opened only in 1791. Prior to this, the only way of traversing the river was by ferry, to which there are numerous references in both medieval and early modern times. One of the principal streets and gates of the walled city led to the Ferry Quay, named to distinguish it from the Ship Quay which was located a little downstream. (These streets and gates are still so named.) The eccentric but eminently practical 'earl bishop' of Derry, Frederick Augustus Hervey, was the first person to seriously pursue the matter of constructing a bridge. From the late 1760s there was continuous correspondence and debate on the subject. Work finally began in 1789 when the firm of Lemuel Cox and Jonathan Thompson began the construction of a wooden bridge. The firm was based in Boston, Massachusetts, where they had gained considerable experience in the bridging of wide, deep, fast-flowing rivers, such as the Foyle. The bridge was opened to pedestrians in 1790 and was officially opened the following year. It was 1,068 feet long and cost £16,294 6s. It had an opening device to allow boats to pass upstream to the town of Strabane in County Tyrone. This involved the construction of a complicated procedure for dividing and reconnecting the water and, later, the gas pipes which also passed over the bridge. The bridge had a toll-house located at the city end, which often occasioned the jibe that the citizens of the Waterside, unlike those of the city itself, could walk almost the full length of the bridge without having to pay. Derry has a long history of being aware of (and complaining about) discriminatory practices.

The former Carlisle Bridge.

By 1863 this wooden bridge had to be replaced. The new Carlisle Bridge was built of iron and, unusually, had two decks. The lower level was used for connecting the various railway networks which, by then, had set up terminuses on both sides of the river. The new bridge facilitated the development of additional suburbs on the south side of the walled city as well as on the Waterside. In 1933 the Carlisle Bridge was replaced by a similar two-level structure named, controversially, after the first Prime Minister of Northern Ireland, Lord Craigavon. By the 1960s the complex railway network emanating from Derry had been reduced to just one line to Belfast and the lower deck of the bridge was altered to carry road traffic as well.

Craigavon Bridge.

One of the most important infrastructure developments for the city in recent times, the construction of a second bridge, the Foyle Bridge, was financed principally from European Union funds. The location chosen was downstream, north of the city, near the site of the famous 'boom' built across the river during the Siege of Derry in 1689. The main structural elements of the Foyle Bridge had been prefabricated in the shipyards of Harland and Wolff in Belfast Harbour and floated on gigantic barges around the coast to their final destination. When it opened in 1984 the Foyle Bridge was the longest bridge in Ireland.

THE AMELIA EARHART COTTAGE

Amelia Earhart was the first woman to fly across the Atlantic. On that occasion she had been a passenger in a plane piloted by men. She resolved to undertake the challenge to fly solo and on 21May 1932 set out from Harbour Grace, Newfoundland. She intended to fly to

Paris in imitation of the pioneering flight of Charles Lindbergh, but as she approached the European coastline on the following day her Lockheed Vega airplane began to run out of fuel. She decided to set down at the first available landing place and began to follow a railway line. Sometime later she put down at Ballyarnett, then an entirely rural area to the north of Derry city, close to the border with the Irish Free State. She was greeted by a number of local people who had been attracted by the sound and sight of her brilliant red airplane. There are many humorous stories about the first words exchanged between the intrepid aviator and the locals. The mayor, Sir Dudley McCorkell, arrived and Miss Earhart posed for photographs. The field where she landed is now inside a public park in a northern suburb of the city, and a small interpretative centre there tells something of the story of this extraordinary woman and the serendipity of her connection with Derry.

THE RIVER FOYLE

Flowing through Derry in a beautiful serpentine, the river Foyle (Irish: *Feabhal*) is now about a thousand feet wide, fast-flowing and, at high tide, about forty feet deep. It is possible to walk alongside the river (a lot of it through parkland), for much of its length as it flows through the built-up urban area. Just below the old walled city the river widens, eventually opening up on its eastern side into Rosse's Bay which is one and a quarter miles wide. From here the river narrows into its final channel before passing Culmore Point, about four miles below the city, where it opens out again, merging into the sea lough with which it shares its name. In all, the river is about twenty miles long, being formed upstream between the towns of Lifford (County Donegal) and Strabane (County Tyrone) by the junction of the rivers Mourne and Finn. In Irish these rivers were known as 'na trí namad' (the three enemies), and the point where they joined together was known as Port na Trí Namad. This probably reflects the fact that the Foyle is tidal right up to this point and, at high water, the three rivers literally do 'fight' each other.

The river and the lough take their name from a mythical character, Feabhal mac Lódain, who is said to have been one of the semi-divine people known as the Tuatha Dé Danann. The lough is said to have erupted suddenly, drowning Feabhal and casting his body ashore but, at the same time, throwing up a large boulder which would become his burial monument.

In many ways the river can be said to be the *raison d'être* of the city. In ancient times it formed a distinctive tribal boundary between the peoples on its east and west banks. Early fortifications and monasteries in Ireland were often located on just such boundaries. In earlier prehistoric times we know, from archaeological finds, that the earliest human colonists in Ireland, the hunter-gatherers of the Mesolithic period (c.7,000 BC to c. 4,000 BC), travelled into the interior of the island along this and similar rivers. In medieval and early modern times, before a good network of roads was established, the Foyle served as a water highway into the heartlands of Gaelic Ulster and was one of the avenues by which this territory was eventually conquered by the English during the reign of Queen Elizabeth I.

The river Foyle at Derry.

During the Siege of Derry in 1689 control of the river became the key to victory. Initially, the Jacobite besiegers blocked the river with a floating barricade or 'boom'. Final victory for the besieged city came only when the Williamite relief ships were able to smash this obstacle and sail up to the city. The location of the port of Derry so far to the west was of immense importance to its growth as a point of embarkation and destination, especially for transatlantic trading and emigration ships of the eighteenth and nineteenth centuries. This strategic importance was exploited again during the Second World War when Derry became a major allied communications, refuelling and repair base as well as 'the most important escort base in the North-Western approaches'. Its importance to allied success in the Battle of the Atlantic was marked by the decision to nominate a surrender point for German U-boats at Lisahally harbour, just below the city, in 1945.

Although ships are a rare sight nowadays on the city's historic quays, the success of the modern port located downstream at the former wartime harbour at Lisahally is an indication of the continuing debt that the city owes to the river Foyle.

TILLIE AND HENDERSON'S FACTORY
AND THE DERRY SHIRT INDUSTRY

As you cross Craigavon Bridge from the Waterside, heading into the city, there is a large industrial building on your left-hand side. Built in a slightly grandiose French château-like style it is the former Tillie and Henderson's shirt-factory, opened in 1857. The Glasgow shirt and collar manufacturer William Tillie and his partner, John Henderson, were the first to introduce the portable sewing machine (recently developed in America), to Derry in the 1850s. The original hand-sewing and cottage-based shirt industry had begun in Derry in the 1830s, based on the local traditional craft of 'sprigging' – white embroidery on a white linen background. Shirt-making was established in Derry by the local Scott family and had proven immensely successful, encouraging outside industrialists, many of them from Scotland, to get involved. The application of steam-powered sewing, and the combination of a cottage-based organisation together with a factory system, allowed the industry to grow, in local terms, to an unparalleled extent.

The Derry shirt industry, and specifically Tillie and Henderson's factory, was mentioned by no less an authority than Karl Marx in *Das Kapital*, as part of his discussion of the transition from work in the domestic setting to the practices of the industrial age. The industry continued to grow and by the 1920s, when it reached its peak, employed about 18,000 people from the city and the surrounding district. Ninety percent of these workers were women, giving a distinctive character to the employment and unemployment profile of the city, not to mention its related sociology. The city is dotted with large, and now largely abandoned, nineteenth-century shirt-factory buildings, many of them constructed in elegant and varying architectural styles as their owners tried to outdo each other. The problem of how to find modern uses for these buildings has yet to be tackled. The shirt industry still survives in a much more limited way, but the last of the city centre factories (called simply The City Factory) has only recently been closed.

THE HARBOUR MUSEUM

In 1996 the former Londonderry Port and Harbour Commissioners Office was converted into the Harbour Museum. The port, along with its commissioners, had moved downstream to a new site at Lisahally, a refurbished old wartime harbour, leaving their beautiful old building beside the Guildhall available for public and civic use. The slightly Italianate-style building, constructed in 1880, is a little older than its imposing municipal neighbour. Originally it would have looked out onto a very busy port but, while wonderful views of the river can still be had from its first floor windows, it is rare nowadays for ships to come this far upriver.

The building has been preserved for the most part in its late nineteenth-century style. Much of the original furniture and fittings, such as the chandeliers and specially-made Killybegs carpet, have been retained, as have many of the portraits of past members – the great and the good of the city who served on the harbour authority in its heyday. The building is full of memorabilia associated with the port and the

Emigration sculpture at Waterloo Place.

river, and also serves as the headquarters of the city's Heritage and Museum Service, along with the municipal archives.

The Iona Currach in the The Harbour Museum.

Among the most interesting items to be seen in the museum is the Iona Currach, a traditional boat sailed from Derry to Iona (the Hebridean island where St Colmcille founded his famous monastery), by a party of Church of Ireland laymen and clerics in 1963 to mark the 1400th anniversary of the original event. Also to be seen is the figurehead and nameplates of the *Minnehaha*, one of the best-loved of Derry's nineteenth-century sailing ships. The former Harbour Commissioners' boardroom is dominated by G. Folingsby's painting of *The Relief of Derry* (c.1863). This picture almost acquired the status of an icon for the Protestant population of the city. In the second half of the last century and the earlier part of this one, it was reproduced in numerous lithographs and prints and hung in many private homes as well as in public buildings. The Harbour Museum provides a poignant and memorable glimpse into aspects of Derry's past which are now totally gone.

VIEWS

One of the classic views of Derry is to be obtained from various locations in the Gobnascale area of the Waterside district of the city. The hillside here rises to above 300 feet and overlooks the river, the hill on which the old city itself is located and the surrounding hills and mountains, most of which are located in County Donegal in the

Republic of Ireland. The distinctive S-shaped curve of the river Foyle as it passes through the city can be seen and, in the distance, Lough Foyle itself is visible. This view of the city has been memorialised in innumerable paintings, prints and photographs since the eighteenth century.

The walled city from the Creggan.

On the western side of the city, across the Bogside valley, rises Creggan Hill. From various places in this area stunning views can be had of the walled city sitting 'fortified' on its hilltop location, as it has done since the plantation at the beginning of the seventeenth century. In some respects this view has not really changed since Thomas Phillips's famous drawing, made in 1685.

Marvellous views over the city and the surrounding countryside can also be had from the restaurant on the top floor of Austin's Department Store at the Diamond in the centre of the town.

THE WORKHOUSE

Derry's newest museum, opened in 1998, is located in part of the former workhouse in the Waterside area of the city. The building was opened originally on 10 November 1840, with accommodation for 800 inmates. It was constructed shortly before the Great Famine, along with similar institutions all over Ireland, to house the destitute. The

The workhouse.

conditions for the inmates in these workhouses were no more than a bare improvement on the extreme misery they had left outside. The regime of the workhouse was organised so as to encourage those who had entered to leave as quickly as possible. On entering, the inmates were stripped of their clothes and any personal possessions, segregated according to age and sex and were required to wear a prison-like uniform. There was compulsory labour which, according to a contemporary instruction, 'should be of a nature as to be irksome and to awaken or increase a dislike to remain in the workhouse'.

The workhouse continued to function, at least to some extent, until 1947 when it became a hospital. That hospital closed down in the late 1980s but, as many of the original workhouse buildings had been preserved, it was decided to develop a small museum on the site.

The main workhouse building has been refurbished and given modern facilities, with a local branch library located on the ground floor. However, the two top floors of the building have been preserved, for the most part, in their original state. Sections of the male and female dormitories can be visited and give some idea of the penitential regime operated in the institution. Ancillary displays outline the local history of the Waterside area of the city. The building also houses an exhibition (first displayed in 1995), to mark the important role the city played in the events of the Second World War.

ST COLUMB'S HALL

St Columb's Hall, built just outside the city walls in Newmarket Street, was opened in 1888 as a Temperance establishment – a 'palace of abstinence' as one commentator called it. It was constructed by a buoyant Catholic community as its chief gathering and entertainment place, to some extent in opposition to the 'Protestant' Corporation Hall and the recently constructed Apprentice Boys' Memorial Hall. The hall, which is a classical Victorian public building, now contains a number of arts and cultural facilities including a large theatre/assembly hall, a small cinema and the Orchard Gallery – a distinguished contemporary visual arts venue operated by the City Council. Despite the fact that the hall is still crowned by a statue of the figure of Temperance (along with Erin and Vulcan), the building now also houses a fully licensed public house.

AUSTIN'S DEPARTMENT STORE

Austin's Department Store in the Diamond, the central square of the walled city, is one of the best-known landmarks in Derry. It was constructed in 1906 following a disastrous fire on the site, which also destroyed the former Corporation Hall in the centre of the square. It is a traditional, elegant department store and claims to be the oldest such institution in Ireland. The external appearance of the building is flamboyant, Edwardian 'wedding cake' style. The main tower of the building with its great bronze cupola is visible from near and far, especially when lit up at Christmas. Marvellous views over the city and the surrounding countryside can be had from the restaurant on the top floor of the building.

THE PLAYHOUSE

The Playhouse is an arts and cultural activity centre located in one of the former girls' school buildings in the centre of the city – the Convent of Mercy school built in 1911. The building has been partly renovated and there are major plans for further improvements and expansion. It is now home to a large range of projects and facilities

The Playhouse.

for cultural and (in the widest sense) educational development. These include a small studio theatre and the Context Gallery – a visual arts venue which is rapidly establishing an important reputation.

THE VERBAL ARTS CENTRE

The Verbal Arts Centre is also currently located in a former city centre school – the Cathedral Primary School built in 1891. The centre is dedicated to the presentation and development of verbal, artistic and cultural expression, be that spoken, written or even sung. Various projects and events are organised across a range of disciplines including drama, poetry, prose literature and storytelling. The centre will be moving from its present location beside St Columb's Cathedral to a newly refurbished venue in the former First Derry Presbyterian School built in 1894. This school had its origins in the older 'Blue Coat' school, founded in 1773, which got its name from the fact that the boy pupils led the singing in the nearby First Derry Presbyterian Church, in return for which they were educated and clothed. The new venue will provide the Centre with a marvellous location, fronting onto the city walls at the Double Bastion, overlooking the Bogside.

THE FOYLE VALLEY RAILWAY MUSEUM

Although only one railway line now runs into Derry, in 1900 there were four separate networks with terminals in the city. Two of these, the Midland Railway which ran to Belfast (still surviving as Northern Ireland Railways), and the former Great Northern Railway which connected the city to Dublin, operated on normal standard gauge lines. The other two systems, the County Donegal Railway and the Londonderry and Lough Swilly Railway operated on the Irish narrow gauge system. The latter company still operates from the city, nowadays as a bus service. It is often jokingly said that it must be one of the few railway companies in the world that has no trains! These four networks, plus a small dockside system, were linked across the river Foyle via the underdeck of the unusual two-tier bridge. By the 1950s this elaborate system had been reduced to its present limited service.

In 1989 the City Council, in association with the North West of Ireland Railway Society, opened the Foyle Valley Railway Museum to tell the story of this fascinating piece of transport history. As well as the static museum which houses a large collection of memorabilia, the building serves as the 'station' for a pleasure railway which runs for about two miles alongside the river Foyle. Railcars of the former County Donegal Railway (a company which was a pioneer in the use of petrol and diesel fuelled locomotives), take visitors along a scenic route which follows part of the permanent way of the former Great Northern system. The Society is constantly extending the line and its facilities and recently a similar group on the other side of the border in County Donegal has initiated plans for a link-up.

THE STORY OF HALF-HANGED MCNAGHTEN
AND PREHEN HOUSE

One of the most beautiful and fascinating objects on display in the Tower Museum is the eighteenth-century Knox carriage, a type of horse-drawn vehicle known as a 'travelling chariot'. In the mid-eighteenth century the Knox family occupied Prehen House, which is still standing. Prehen is now the name of one of the suburbs of the city on the east bank of the river Foyle. The name is an anglicisation of the Irish word *préachán* meaning 'a crow'. It was derived from the rookeries in the woods surrounding the house, which was designed by a local architect, Michael Priestley, about 1745. The house is still a private residence but it can be seen, beautifully framed by its surroundings, from the west bank of the river south of the city, particularly from the Foyle Valley Railway Museum train.

In the eighteenth century the house was occupied by Andrew Knox, a member of the Irish Parliament for County Donegal. Andrew had a beautiful young daughter, Mary Anne. She was just fifteen years of age when, in 1761, she met the notorious gambler John McNaghten who had formerly been sheriff for County Antrim. Despite his questionable reputation, Andrew Knox felt sorry for McNaghten and invited him to Prehen. Depending on the version of the story, McNaghten either fell hopelessly in love with Mary Anne or saw her inheritance as his chance of salvation but, at any rate, he determined to marry her. He cajoled her into reading through the marriage service and, on this basis, claimed her as his wife. Andrew Knox was outraged and forbade any contact between the couple. The wily McNaghten is said to have flouted this injunction, repeatedly going to the house in disguise.

Whatever the facts, McNaghten won the support of many of the local people including, it is said, some of the servants of the house who helped him in his subterfuge. He made plans to abduct Mary Anne and, although he failed on his first attempt, he proposed to hold up her father's coach when she was accompanying him on one occasion when he was going to Parliament in Dublin. On the morning

The Knox carriage, Tower Museum.

of 10 November 1761, McNaghten lay in wait in the woods at Clough-cor, on the road to Strabane. However, in the débâcle which ensued when he tried to stop the coach, Mary Anne was shot dead. When McNaghten was eventually tracked down, tried and found guilty, popular sympathy for him ensured that, at first, no one could be found to build the gallows from which he was to be hanged. Not only that, but when he was eventually brought to the gallows the rope broke, allowing an opportunity for him to escape. Incredibly, McNaghten returned, saying that he did not wish to be known as 'the half-hanged man'. The rope held the second time and he died. Unfortunately for McNaghten, he has always been dubbed with the very epithet he so valiantly tried to avoid.

MAGEE COLLEGE

Magee College is now part of the University of Ulster, an institution established in 1984 by the merging of four previously separate third level colleges: the main New University of Ulster campus at Coleraine, the Ulster Polytechnic at Jordanstown in County Antrim, the Art College in Belfast and the old Magee College itself which, since the 1960s, had been a satellite institution of the New University of Ulster. As early as 1845 the authorities in Derry had lobbied the then British Prime Minister, Sir Robert Peel, requesting that the city should be the location of one of the three new Queen's Colleges (dubbed at the time by their opponents as the 'Godless colleges'), being set up in various parts of Ireland. However, on that occasion, the college for the north of Ireland was established in Belfast.

Magee was originally set up in 1865 as a Presbyterian theological and liberal arts college. It is named after Mrs Martha Magee, the wife of a Dublin Presbyterian minister whose bequest of £20,000 helped establish the college. The main Gothic-style buildings date from that period as do several of the adjoining college houses which are named after a number of the distinguished nineteenth-century college professors. Although steeped in Presbyterian tradition, Magee had a fairly liberal reputation from the outset. At the college foundation ceremony in 1856, one of the trustees promised that

> 'no surly janitor [door-keeper] shall stand at the gate to say to men of any denomination, Here is a fountain of science and piety at which you may not drink.'

The arrival of Magee College provided an impetus for the development of the intellectual life of the city in the second half of the nineteenth century. Among the more interesting members of its faculty was the Reverend Professor Thomas Witherow, whose writings on the Siege of Derry and associated events still repay the reader. Magee remained a relatively small institution. But following the reorganisation of university education in Ireland in 1908 (in several ways prefiguring the partition of the country thirteen years later), Magee developed a relationship with Trinity College in Dublin which endured until the 1960s.

At that time, the government of Northern Ireland set about establishing a second independent university alongside Queen's University, Belfast. It is often claimed that the political manoeuvres surrounding this issue lead to the politicisation of the nationalist or Catholic population of the city. This eventually was to erupt in the civil rights movement at the outset of the Troubles, leading to the eventual collapse of the Northern Ireland government. At the time, it was widely assumed that Magee and Derry would become the location for the new university. However, when the decision was eventually made that it would be situated in Coleraine instead, nationalists became convinced that the unionist government was not prepared to establish any institution which could bring economic and social benefits to the 'Catholic city' of Derry. Feelings about this were strengthened when it became known that some unionists in the city (the so-called 'faceless men'), were secretly conniving with the government in Belfast about this issue.

Magee College.

In view of this, it is interesting to note that in the 1850s, prior to the establishment of Magee College, there was considerable debate as to where that college should be located. The choice on that occasion also fell between Derry and the town of Coleraine, thirty-five miles to the north, but Derry was successful at that time. The 1960s 'university for Derry' campaign, which aroused considerable cross-community support and activity, brought to outside attention several individuals who would figure in the events leading to the outbreak of the Troubles and the events thereafter. Not least of these was John Hume.

The New University of Ulster was set up with its main campus at Coleraine. Magee, which became affiliated to it, slipped into a secondary role. It developed a significant reputation in the field of adult and continuing education, not least in the field of 'second chance' education for mature students. The 1980s brought more organisational upheaval with the 'merger' which led to the establishing of the University of Ulster. Magee was given a considerably enhanced role in this institution. Its courses, student and staff numbers, and its building and resource provisions were all improved. From the few hundred students of the 1970s numbers have now swelled to over two thousand and the college seems set for a less controversial, but more positive, phase in its history. Arising from its location in an area beset with inter-communal conflict, Magee has set up a number of Peace Study programmes and has also developed a relationship with the United Nations university.

THE TOWER MUSEUM

By the late 1970s the centre of Derry had been virtually destroyed. It was claimed that about 30 percent of the 'downtown' area had been bombed or burnt out, and a combination of economic avoidance and official neglect meant that much of the remaining 70 percent was in very poor condition. Paddy Doherty, a well-known community activist from the Bogside, spearheaded the establishment of a number of inter-related organisations designed both to improve the job prospects of the city's unemployed youth and, simultaneously, to rebuild the shattered inner city. When Doherty learned about the 'reconstruction' of the American historic town of Williamsburg in Virginia, he began to think that something along these lines might be feasible in Derry.

Apart from its physical disintegration, there was a profound cultural disregard for the historic walled centre of Derry or, as it should be more correctly named in this instance, Londonderry. As a result of the Troubles and the demographic shifts of the early to mid-1970s, the city's Protestant population had abandoned this historic area and the Catholic population hadn't yet taken responsibility for it. By using the city's seventeenth-century surrounding walls as a metaphor, saying that they could be regarded as either 'a noose or a necklace', Doherty began to focus attention on the importance of the city's physical legacy. It would be true to say that conservationists had been arguing this point for some time, but it had been seen up to then as a middle class issue exclusively. Doherty widened the social appeal of the suggestion by linking it directly to the issue of job creation and the exploitation of that heritage as an economic resource.

One of the ideas put forward by Doherty was the 'reconstruction' of the O'Doherty Castle which had been erected in Derry in late medieval times. In fact, the building in question had actually belonged to a more powerful local family, the O'Donnells, but it had been built for them by their underlings, the O'Dohertys, after the latter had bought the site for the princely sum of 'twenty cows'. The construction of the plantation city of Londonderry in the seventeenth century had effectively obliterated most of the structures which had survived from Gaelic times. Thus, there was no Gaelic/nationalist/'Catholic' monument to be pointed out as the equivalent of the English/unionist/ arguably 'Protestant' city walls. The balance, however, could be redressed by 'rebuilding' such a monument.

The struggle to build this enigmatic structure acquired almost mythical status. It was a classic 'them and us' situation: the man in the street versus the bureaucratic expert, second city Derry versus an

Tower Museum, Bishop Hervey plans the city's first bridge.

uncaring Belfast and, despite efforts at cross-community involvement, there were even hints of the ancient struggle between people
from the 'native' tradition versus those from a 'colonist' background.
The story of how Paddy Doherty acquired the alleged site (but almost
certainly *not* the site) of the original castle for the building, is itself
the stuff of legend. It was owned by a London businessman of Jewish
background. The latter tried to avoid the requested meeting with
Doherty but, having failed in this, he argued that he could only
charge the market price for the site or give it away as a gift. He was
eventually persuaded to part with the site for a peppercorn price.
Doherty then persuaded the City Council to take on the project
(after his organisation had sold the site on to the Council allegedly
for considerably more than the peppercorn sum he had paid for it).
After considerable modification of the original plan to ensure that
the building would more closely resemble an Irish tower-house castle
of the relevant period, work began on the structure using European
Regional Development Fund money. It was completed in 1986.

It was envisaged that the building would be used as some sort of
heritage centre. Doherty and his organisation had continued with
their original plans of reconstructing the inner city. Another development at the rear of the mock castle, the craft village, allowed for a
huge space to be created underground which could be linked to the
tower. By this stage, the City Council's Heritage and Museum Service
had a new vision for the site, planning an innovative museum which
would integrate the presentation techniques of the heritage centre
approach with the conservation professionalism of the traditional
museum – the Tower Museum was born.

The Tower Museum (or more correctly phase one of it), was
opened to the public in October 1992. As it had to deal with a controversial subject (the history of a very ancient but divided city), it was
extremely important that it should receive the approval of both sections of the community. Expectations that it would have a nationalist
bias were quickly quashed on the day of its official opening when no
less a person than the Reverend Ian Paisley, who attended in his
capacity as a member of the European Parliament, declared that 'it
was the best history museum [he had] seen'.

The museum has a deliberate narrative approach. The 'story' of
the city is told using a combination of theatrical devices, audio-visual
programmes and archaeological and historical objects from all

The O'Doherty Tower.

periods of its past – from the arrival of the first humans to the area in the Mesolithic period (c.7,000 BC), to the most recent events of the Troubles and subsequent regeneration. The Tower Museum has the unique distinction of being the only institution ever to have been both Irish and British Museum of the Year. When it came joint-second in the European Museum of the Year Awards in 1994, the judges praised the museum for attempting to be 'a bridge between [the] political and religious factions in Northern Ireland, a function it has fulfilled with conspicuous success'.

The museum has enjoyed huge popular success because of, and not, as some predicted, in spite of, its upfront treatment of the contemporary Northern Ireland conflict and the historical events which inform it. Over the next two years the museum will be completing phase two of its exhibits – a display of materials from the Spanish Armada ship *La Trinidad Valencera*, which was identified and excavated by members of the City of Derry Sub-Aqua Club in the early 1970s, one of the few 'good news' stories to come out of the city at that time.

A NAME: DERRY OR LONDONDERRY

On 29 March 1613 Derry became Londonderry by a charter of King James I. Nine years earlier, on 11 July 1604, the same king had created, by another charter, the 'free, entire, and perfect city and county of itself, to be called the city and county of Derrie ...' A lot had happened during those intervening years. The city's status had allowed a small colonial trading settlement to develop which included among its burgesses the local Gaelic aristocrat (and the recently ennobled) Sir Cahir O'Doherty. However, relations between the English of Derrie and O'Doherty deteriorated and, in 1608, the latter attacked, by and large destroying 'the poor infant city'.

These events more or less coincided with a change of policy by King James who now sought to 'solve' his version of the Ulster problem by the radical tactic of plantation or massive colonisation. Six of Ulster's counties (but not the six of the present state of Northern Ireland), were deemed to be forfeit to the Crown after 'the flight of the earls', as the departure of the defeated leaders of Gaelic Ulster to the continent came to be known.

The king invited (in fact, forced) the ancient trades' guilds of the City of London to undertake the organisation and financing of part of this plantation scheme. The area assigned to them was the county of Coleraine (the former Gaelic territory known as Oireacht Uí Catháin), together with a number of additional smaller areas including the ancient settlement of Derry.

The new name for that settlement and its associated county, Londonderry, was a recognition of the involvement of the Londoners in this bold scheme. An organisation known as The Society of the Governor and Assistants, London, of the New Plantation in Ulster, within the realm of Ireland was set up to oversee the colonising scheme. It was effectively a subcommittee of the Corporation of the City of London. That body, now usually known by the shorter version of its title – The Honourable The Irish Society, or simply The Irish Society – still exists and is still the ground landlord for much of the area of the city. However, it devotes most of its income to local philanthropic schemes.

The 1613 change of the name of the city was recognised in all the subsequent charters and relevant municipal legislation down to modern times, including the reforms of 1973 (resulting from the onset of the Troubles), which set up Londonderry City Council. In 1984, however, the Council obtained permission from the government to change its name (but not that of the city), to Derry City Council. Apart from any other considerations, a request to change the name of the city itself would have required what is known as a Loyal Address to Queen Elizabeth, something which, to say the least, would not have been too easy for the, by then, nationalist-controlled body. The technical, legal and official situation, therefore, is that Londonderry City is run by Derry City Council. However, it can hardly be doubted that for the overwhelming majority of the people who actually live there, Derry is Derry.

'Derry' is an anglicisation of the old Irish word *daire* (modern Irish: *doire*) which seems to mean something like 'the oak grove'. In both its Gaelic and anglicised versions it is a very common place name element in Ireland – over a thousand distinct instances, at least, are known – indicating the prevalence and importance of oak trees in the economy and ritual life of the country during the pre-modern period. Interestingly, there is a sword in the Tower Museum, given as a gift to the city from the City of London in 1616, which includes in its pommel inscription a reference to L*O*N*D*O*N*D*E*R*R*E. It seems that this peculiar spelling of the latter part of the name is an attempt to render the Irish pronunciation of the Gaelic word *doire*. However, as early as May 1605, Mrs Montgomery, in a letter noting that her husband had just been appointed first Protestant Bishop of 'Derye', added 'I pray God may make us all merry'. Presumably she was making a rhyme with the, by then accepted, English pronunciation of the name.

As far back as our records go (whether in Latin, Irish or English), the name of the city has always included a reference to oak trees in some combination or variation of spelling; in fact, over fifty such variations are known. The oldest known name for the place was Daire Calgach. The second element seems to mean something like 'fierce' or 'sharp'. This was almost certainly a masculine, personal name, however, the identity of the man concerned is not known. If he was a real person rather than a legendary character, he must have lived earlier than the early seventh century when the name first appears in contemporary records. A Latin version of this name, Roboretum Calgachi, also occurs in seventh-century documentation. It seems that by about the eleventh century the second part of the name, Calgach, was dropped. From at least the early twelfth century it became common to add the name of the distinguished early Irish saint, Colmcille, who was believed to have founded a Christian monastery in the city in the sixth century.

Derry is by no means the only place in Europe where, for different linguistic, ethnic or political reasons, a choice of names exist and where the use of a name can indicate a particular point of view. Sometimes, as in the case of Derry, the official response to a situation like this can be slightly ridiculous. The BBC (British Broadcasting Corporation), for instance, enforces a policy whereby the first reference to the city in any exchange must be to Londonderry. This can lead to all sorts of awkward situations, such as the deliberate misquoting of their sources. Various compromises have been proposed over the years to try to resolve this issue once and for all. It has been suggested that Derry become the official name of the city and Londonderry the name of the county. Another idea is that the name Londonderry be retained in the city as a district name for the historic walled area – the original seventeenth-century Londonderry. None of these 'academic' solutions have found popular support and the ad hoc situation remains. On the positive side, however, an increasing awareness of the complexity and richness of all aspects of the city's heritage is opening up new possibilities. Perhaps the day will come when, instead of being a controversial issue, people will say of this place, as of New York, New York, 'so good they named it twice'.

THE FORMER ST COLUMB'S COLLEGE
(NOW LUMEN CHRISTI COLLEGE)

In the late eighteenth century the then Church of Ireland (Protestant) Bishop of Derry, Frederick Augustus Hervey, built a house called *Casino* on a high part of the hill of Derry, just outside the city, despite the fact that there was an Episcopal palace nearby, within the walls. Bishop Hervey, an all-round man of the Enlightenment, if something of an eccentric, was also the Earl of Bristol, the so-called 'earl bishop'. Among the many qualities and benefits which he brought to the diocese and city of Derry were his religious tolerance and ecumenism. Thus, there was something of an appropriateness when, late in the nineteenth century, *Casino* was sold to the Catholic church authorities.

Lumen Christi College.

In 1879 'St Columkille's Church and Derry Diocesan Seminary at Casino, Londonderry' was opened on the site of the 'earl bishop's' residence. Close to the main college buildings and to the former bishop's house are the remains of a seventeenth-century windmill tower. For a while the tower, minus its sails, had served the purpose of a dovecote for the house. The windmill is shown most elaborately on a drawing of Derry by Thomas Phillips made in 1685. Four years later, during the Siege of Derry, the environs of the tower was the location for one of the set battles of the siege. On the night of 5 May the Jacobite besiegers of the city captured and fortified the windmill. However, on the following day, the city's defenders sallied out and recaptured the area, inflicting heavy casualties on the Jacobites and capturing two bright yellow French banners. The renewed remains of these banners are still displayed in St Columb's Cathedral.

In what might well have been some sort of echo of this event of the seventeenth century, on the night of 21 June 1920, during a period of major inter-communal violence in the city associated with the moves towards the partition of Ireland, members of the (Protestant) Ulster Volunteer Force (UVF), attempted to take control of the windmill and the adjoining buildings. On that occasion the IRA were successful in recapturing the area.

Despite these violent associations, the buildings on the site are now more especially connected with the history of one of the city's main educational institutions, St Columb's College. That college has now moved to another location and a very new school has taken its place, but St Columb's will undoubtedly be remembered for its astonishing number of internationally successful students from the post-1947 Education Reform Act period. These include: John Hume, Seamus Heaney, Seamus Deane, Brian Friel, Phil Coulter and Eamonn McCann, as well as a host of other celebrated Derrymen. As has been pointed out repeatedly, there can be few schools in the world which have produced *two* Nobel prizewinners.

The grounds also contained the location of another of Derry's famous Catholic schools of former years, the Christian Brothers' Brow of the Hill.

'FREE DERRY' CORNER

One of the most momentous events in the early history of the Troubles occurred on Saturday, 4 January 1969. Despite calls from moderate nationalists for a truce in the wake of a series of protests which had been mounting since the famous march in Derry on 5 October 1968, a group from the People's Democracy, a radical leftist organisation set up at Queen's University, Belfast, set out on a four day march to Derry on New Year's Day 1969. The marchers were constantly harassed en route but, as they made their way along the last few miles into Derry, they were viciously attacked by loyalists at Burntollett Bridge.

It was alleged that there had been collusion between the attackers and members of the police force, the RUC (Royal Ulster Constabulary). The marchers eventually got through to the city and, as their stories were told, serious rioting against the police commenced. At 2.00am on the following Sunday morning, a group of policemen invaded the Catholic Bogside area of the city and wreaked havoc. A government commission was set up to investigate what had happened and found that the police had been guilty of substantial 'misconduct which involved assault and battery, malicious damage to property ... and the use of provocative sectarian and political slogans ...' On the following day vigilante squads were set up in the Bogside and a well-known local character, John 'Caker' Casey, painted the famous slogan on the gable wall of one of the terraces of houses: 'You are now entering Free Derry', in imitation of a similar slogan in West Berlin. The giant slogan became a focal point for the outdoor meetings and rallies which became a regular part of Bogside life in the coming years.

Although the actual terrace of houses has long since gone, the gable wall and its slogan have been preserved. It is still the venue for many public meetings. Over the years the slogan has often been damaged by tins of paint thrown at it by frustrated members of the security forces. It has been repainted in various forms on many occasions and other evocative symbols have often been attached to it. In recent years it has also become the practice to paint additional images and slogans on the reverse of the wall signifying and celebrating local community events. That gable wall with its defiant slogan has become one of the most enduring images of the Troubles and of the Bogside area of Derry.

THE APPRENTICE BOYS' MEMORIAL HALL

The Memorial Hall (or as it is known locally 'the Mem'), is the headquarters of the Apprentice Boys of Derry organisation, one of the so-called 'loyal' institutions. Unlike its fellow Protestant organisations, such as the Orange Order or the Black Preceptory, the Apprentice Boys have as their only function the continuation of the memory of the 'brave thirteen' original 'apprentice boys' who, on 7 December 1688, shut the gates of the city against the advance of soldiers loyal

Plaque announcing the Apprentice Boys'
Memorial Hall.

to the Catholic king, James II, thus instigating the events which led to the Siege of Derry. The modern Apprentice Boys are best known to the public through their annual parades in December and August which, in the past, have often been accompanied by major controversy and opposition from some sections of the Catholic community.

Much of the building, which was constructed in antiquarian Baronial style, dates to 1873 and was designed by John Guy Ferguson, a well-known local architect, Apprentice Boy and controversial public figure; the Hall was extended in 1937. The building contains private lodge and meeting rooms, leisure facilities, a small museum and a large assembly hall. Next to it is a small memorial garden which is dominated by the statue of Governor Walker, one of the heroes of the siege. The statue originally stood on top of a tall pillar (reminiscent of Nelson's Column), which was located on the city walls overlooking the Bogside. The pillar, which was a well-known if controversial landmark, was deliberately destroyed by bomb-blast in 1973 in what was almost certainly a purely tribal exercise in 'totem pole' destruction.

Throughout the eighteenth century there were several groups named after the original Apprentice Boys. The present organisation was founded in 1813 in Dublin and its Derry section was established the following year. Subsequently, Derry became the home of the organisation and now new initiates can only be properly sworn in within the seventeenth-century walls of the city. Although membership of the organisation is restricted to Protestant males, in recent years, through various festival events, the Apprentice Boys have courageously begun to open their activities to wider participation. Their aim in so doing is to move on from the controversies of the past, to promote greater civic harmony and to encourage an unbiased appreciation of the actual historical events of 1688 and 1689.

THE GRIANÁN OF AILEACH AND ELAGHMORE

On the north-western outskirts of the city, just inside the boundary with County Donegal, lie the very partial remains of a small medieval castle at a place called Elaghmore. The castle may have been built about the fourteenth century by the O'Doherty family, the lords of the Inishowen peninsula which stretches away to the north. The

O'Dohertys also built a small castle in Derry itself for their overlords, the O'Donnells, probably around the year 1500. Elaghmore is an anglicisation of the Irish name Aileach Mór, meaning Big or Great Aileach. Aileach was the name of one of the main kingdoms of the north-west of Ireland in early medieval times, that is, from about the sixth to the twelfth century. At its greatest, the kingdom included much of the territory of the modern counties of Derry, Donegal and Tyrone, as well as some other adjacent areas. The name is best commemorated at the great hilltop site now known as the Grianán of Aileach, which overlooks Elaghmore and is about four miles west of Derry. Here there is a complex of ancient monuments extending far back into the prehistoric period.

The interior of the Grianán of Aileach.

The Grianán of Aileach is mentioned frequently in the ancient literature of Ireland as one of the chief residences of the people known as the northern Uí Néill – the northern families who claimed descent from the legendary hero, Niall of the Nine Hostages. Some scholars have argued that Elaghmore is the proper location of that site but modern consensus would favour the better-known Grianán of Aileach. This is located on the summit of an 800-foot high hill which overlooks Lough Swilly and Lough Foyle, as well as much of the neighbouring countryside. The site is dominated by a great circular, stone fortification (a cashel), which seems to date to the early medieval period. The interior of the fort rises in terraces. The steps are easily climbed and afford astonishing views of the surrounding landscape.

This fortification stands near the centre of a series of low rise, concentric earthen banks which are now are all but buried from view by heather. The two outermost banks seem to belong to a typical hillfort of the Iron Age or Late Bronze Age and may date back as far as 1,000 BC. The earliest monument on the hilltop seems to have been a tumulus or prehistoric burial mound which was surveyed early in the last century but has since been destroyed. Compared to similar sites elsewhere in the country, it may be that this mound dated back to the Neolithic period, about 3,000 BC.

Apart from its strong historical background, the Grianán of Aileach is also rich in mythological associations. Some stories claim that it was a royal burial place in ancient times while others state that there is a sleeping army inside the hill waiting to be called forth if needed. Other traditions claim that St Patrick came here in the fifth century – a 'holy well' can be found on the southern edge of the site, between the two outermost earthen banks.

Visitors to the Grianán should not miss the beautiful Catholic church, dedicated to St Aengus, at nearby Burt. The church is located at the foot of the hill on the main road from Derry to Letterkenny, just at the junction of the turnoff for the Grianán itself. The shape of this early circular church (1967), designed by the distinguished Irish architect Liam McCormick, is in part a reflection of the form of the ancient stone fort on top of the hill.